WOMEN AND AGING

by

Ellen M. Gee

Assistant Professor of Sociology
Simon Fraser University

and

Meredith M. Kimball

Associate Professor of Psychology and Women's Studies
Simon Fraser University

Butterworths
Toronto and Vancouver

Women and Aging

Printed and bound in Canada

The Butterworth Group of Companies

Canada
Butterworths, Toronto and Vancouver

United Kingdom
Butterworth & Co. (Publishers) Ltd., London and Edinburgh

Australia
Butterworth Pty Ltd., Sydney, Melbourne, Brisbane, Adelaide and Perth

New Zealand
Butterworths (New Zealand) Ltd., Wellington and Auckland

Singapore
Butterworth & Co. (Asia) Pte. Ltd., Singapore

South Africa
Butterworth Publishers (SA) (Pty) Ltd., Durban and Pretoria

United States
Butterworth Legal Publishers, Boston, Seattle, Austin and St. Paul
D&S Publishers, Clearwater

Canadian Cataloguing in Publication Data

Gee, Ellen Margaret Thomas, 1950-
Women and aging

(Perspectives on individual and population aging)
Bibliography: p.
Includes index.
ISBN 0-409-81152-1

1. Aged women – Canada – Social conditions.
2. Aged women – Canada – Psychology. 3. Aging–
Canada – Social aspects. 4. Aging – Canada –
Psychological aspects. I. Kimball, Meredith M.
II. Title.

HQ1064.C3G43   1987   305.4'0971   C87-093886-X

Executive Editor (P. & A.): Lebby Hines
Sponsoring Editor: Janet Turner
Managing Editor: Linda Kee
Supervisory Editor: Marie Graham
Freelance Projects Coordinator: Joan Chaplin
Editor: Maura Brown
Cover Design: Patrick Ng
Production: Jill Thomson

To the memory of my mother-in-law,
Sue Fong Gee (1907–1986),
whose life was a vivid portrayal of
women's rich interpersonal ties
amid social and economic powerlessness.

E.M.G.

To my grandmothers:
Marie Dillow Fink,
and
Mary Ogg Delzell

M.M.K.

BUTTERWORTHS PERSPECTIVES ON INDIVIDUAL AND POPULATION AGING SERIES

The initiation of this Series represents an exciting and significant development for gerontology in Canada. Since the production of Canadian-based knowledge about individual and population aging is expanding rapidly, students, scholars and practitioners are seeking comprehensive yet succinct summaries of the literature on specific topics. Recognizing the common need of this diverse community of gerontologists, Janet Turner, Sponsoring Editor at Butterworths, conceived the idea of a series of specialized monographs that could be used in gerontology courses to complement existing texts and, at the same time, to serve as a valuable reference for those initiating research, developing policies, or providing services to elderly Canadians.

Each monograph includes a state-of-the-art review and analysis of the Canadian-based scientific and professional knowledge on the topic. Where appropriate for comparative purposes, information from other countries is introduced. In addition, some important policy and program implications of the current knowledge base are discussed, and unanswered policy and research questions are raised to stimulate further work in the area. The monographs have been written for a wide audience: undergraduate students in a variety of gerontology courses; graduate students and research personnel who need a summary and analysis of the Canadian literature prior to initiating research projects; practitioners who are involved in the daily planning and delivery of services to aging adults; and policy-makers who require current and reliable information in order to design, implement and evaluate policies and legislation for an aging population.

The decision to publish a monograph on a specific topic has been based in part on the relevance of the topic for the academic and professional community, as well as on the extent of information available at the time an author is signed to a contract. Thus, not all the conceivable topics are included in the early stages of the Series and some topics are published earlier rather than later. Because gerontology in Canada is attracting large numbers of highly qualified graduate students as well as increasingly active research personnel in academic, public and private settings, new areas of concentrated research will evolve. Hence, additional monographs that review and analyze work in these areas will be needed to reflect the evolution of knowledge on specialized topics pertaining to individual or population aging in Canada.

Before introducing the fifth monograph in the Series, I would like, on behalf of the Series' authors and the gerontology community, to acknowledge the following members of the Butterworths "team" and their respective staffs for their unique and sincere contribution to gerontology in Canada: Geoffrey Burn, President, for his continuing support of the project despite difficult times in the Canadian publishing industry; Janet Turner, Sponsoring Editor, for her vision, endurance and high academic standards; Linda Kee, Managing Editor, for her coordination of the production, especially her constant reminders to authors (and the Series Editor) that the hands of the clock continue to move in spite of our perceptions that manuscript deadlines were still months or years away; Jim Shepherd, Production Manager, for nimbly vaulting many a technical obstacle; and Gloria Vitale, Academic Sales Manager, for her support and promotion of the Series. For each of you, we hope the knowledge provided in this Series will have personal value — but not until well into the next century!

Barry D. McPherson
Series Editor

FOREWORD

As Professor McDaniel (*Canada's Aging Population*) documented in the inaugural monograph in this Series, women constitute an increasing majority of the elderly population in Canada. Moreover, this sex imbalance is projected to increase by the year 2000 from the current ratio of 124 women per 100 men to 134 per 100 for the 65- to 79-year age group, and from 134 to 218 for the 80 and over age group. Clearly, as the previous monographs have shown, age-related processes and problems pertaining to ethnicity, drug use, and crime are especially pronounced among older women. Similarly, when age-related issues such as widowhood, poverty, longevity, health, elder abuse, sexuality, the empty nest, and the "sandwich" generation are discussed, most of these concerns pertain to the situation of middle-aged and elderly women. Unfortunately, though, stereotypes and myths have evolved, whereby middle-aged and older women are perceived to be a homogeneous group with common problems, concerns, and status. In reality, as this monograph documents, there are considerable variations within and between age groups with respect to health, mortality, economic status, sexuality, and the occupational and family life-course experienced by Canadian women.

Employing the perspectives of sociology, demography, psychology, and women's studies, Professors Gee and Kimball critically review and evaluate the social science literature on issues unique to aging women. After introducing the theoretical perspectives and methodological approaches employed in studies of women and aging (Chapter 1), they compare the age-sex structure of the Canadian population and sex differentials in mortality (Chapter 2). Chapters 3 to 7 review and critique the literature concerning the health and economic status, the occupational and family life-course, and the sexuality of middle-aged and elderly women. Throughout, policy implications related to these women's issues and needed research avenues are identified and discussed.

This fifth monograph in the Series represents a comprehensive and important contribution to our understanding of women in the middle and later years of the life-course. Hence, the monograph should be read by practitioners, policy-makers, and professionals who need to understand more fully the aging process for women. As well, students in courses or fields of study such as gerontology, nursing, social work, sociology, women's studies, psychology, and planning, will find this monograph to be an invaluable source of information, as well as one which stimulates thought, debate, and concern about aging as a women's issue.

Finally, it is important to reinforce the comment in the authors' Preface that, although aging for women can be a difficult journey, most women cope well with the hardships and inequalities they experience. At the same time, with increased knowledge and the implementation of scientifically based policies designed specifically to meet women's needs, future cohorts could have an easier journey through the life-course. The authors and I challenge the reader to initiate creative research, policy planning, and program evaluation that will improve the quality of life for future cohorts of middle-aged and elderly Canadian women.

Barry D. McPherson, Ph.D.
Series Editor
Waterloo, Ontario, Canada
June, 1987

PREFACE

The study of women and aging is, of necessity, multi-disciplinary. The academic disciplines of psychology, sociology, economics, demography, political science, biology, chemistry, medicine, etc., all can, and do, make contributions. We cannot include knowledge gleaned from all disciplines in this book, due to our own specialized academic backgrounds and due to time and space constraints. However, we are a multi-disciplinary team, representing sociology and demography (Gee) and psychology and women's studies (Kimball). Thus, this monograph will focus primarily on the sociological and psychological aspects of women and aging. While we will invariably omit research findings from other specialized areas, our coverage is broader than one based on a single discipline.

While aging is a multi-faceted phenomenon, one important aspect of aging is the degree to which it is tied to women's issues. At the level of the individual, women are more likely than men to reach old age, particularly extreme old age. At the societal level, the aged population is increasingly composed of women and will become even more so in future years.

The association of women and aging has not gone unnoticed, and a considerable amount of research has been done, particularly in recent years, on this general topic. Hence, one of our aims is to provide an overview of the social science literature relating to issues that are of importance to women as they age. Our overview contains as much Canadian content as possible. Where Canadian material is not available, we rely on American literature.

However, this monograph represents more than a summary of existing research findings. An imporant second aim here is to critically evaluate the research literature on women and aging on theoretical and/or methodological grounds. In addition, we seek to identify gaps in existing knowledge and, thereby, suggest directions for further research.

Women and aging is a topic that has implications for many facets of our society and our lives, including economic structure, family life, health, and ideology, to list just a few. Thus, a final aim of our book is to identify policy implications that emanate from the research literature.

Chapter 1 provides a discussion of the main psychological and sociological perspectives employed in the study of women and aging, along with a brief examination of methodological issues relevant to our topic. Chapter 2 examines the changing Canadian age-sex structure and discusses the major explanations for women's lower mortality, the main determinant of the increasing "femaleness" of our population, particularly at the older ages. In

Chapter 3, attention is turned to sex differences in health and some selected health concerns of older women. Chapter 4 addresses the issue of poverty among older women, linking it to the economic vulnerability that women face throughout their lives. Aspects of the occupational life-course of women are examined in Chapter 5. In Chapter 6, the family life-course of women is discussed, focussing upon both objective and subjective dimensions. Chapter 7 examines images of older women, particularly the stereotype of the asexual older woman in the light of research related to women's sexuality. Chapter 8 provides suggestions for future research. Chapters 2 through 7 conclude with a section on policy implications related to the respective topics covered in them.

A major theme that emerges from our examination of this literature on women and aging is that women, in spite of their social and economic powerlessness, cope well with aging. As so aptly put by Roebuck (1983, 263), it is older women who are "most likely to teach us ... how *to make the most out of the least* ..." (emphasis added). While we cannot condone the social inequality that women, particularly older women, have to deal with, we think it appropriate to underscore the personal strength that women display throughout their lives and as they age.

ACKNOWLEDGEMENTS

We are indebted to many individuals who helped us in various ways in the writing of this book. We wish to thank Dr. Barry McPherson, the Series Editor, and Janet Turner, Linda Kee and the other editors at Butterworths for their expert advice and support. Dr. Susan McDaniel of the University of Waterloo provided constructive comments on an earlier draft that were greatly appreciated. Dr. Jean Veevers of the University of Victoria provided useful assistance with obtaining references. Also, we wish to thank a number of people affiliated with Simon Fraser University: Lyn Webster of the Department of Computing Science for her help with computer analysis of the Canada Health Survey Tape; Belle Bojanowski of the Gerontology Research Centre for her always willing assistance with our requests in obtaining references; Donna Popovic of the Gerontology Research Centre for patiently and expertly typing and re-typing our revisions; and Dr. Gloria Gutman, Director of the Gerontology Research Centre, for providing funds for typing and photocopying.

We also wish to thank, separately, a number of persons. Ellen Gee thanks her husband, Gordie, for his support and exhibiting the kind and degree of patience that living with a time-pressured and frequently abstracted academic entails; her mother, Margaret Thomas, for her always available ear and her help with childrearing, particularly in the summer and fall of 1986; and her daughter, Adrienne, who can put things into perspective in a way unique to six-year olds. Meredith Kimball wishes to thank the students in her Women and Aging Seminar who first explored much of this material with her; Marvin Fink and Yvonne Mercereau for encouraging responses to earlier drafts; Janet Stoppard for information on depression; Vicky Gray for discussion and encouragement; and the Ancient Mariners for providing stress reduction during the main push to finish the first draft.

CONTENTS

TABLES AND FIGURES

CHAPTER 1

THEORETICAL PERSPECTIVES AND METHODS IN THE STUDY OF WOMEN AND AGING

As a preliminary step in the examination of women and aging, we provide an overview of the main theoretical perspectives[1] employed by psychologists and sociologists in the study of aging. Perspective can be thought of as a lens by which we view a part of the world. It is very important to note that the world is not just "there"; it is seen and interpreted through the perspective that we use. For example, let us say that we observe that women are more prone to depression than men. This observation could be explained in a number of different ways, depending on the perspective we employ. It could be viewed as the result of women's hormones, women's introspective nature, women's greater willingness to admit feeling depressed, or women's devalued social and economic role.

Not only do different perspectives provide different answers to questions, they also determine what questions we ask. For example, if the perspective that is adopted assumes that family is the focal point of women's lives, then issues concerning employment outside the home will tend to be ignored. Also, different perspectives imply different courses of political action and different kinds of social policy. In other words, perspectives are not "neutral"; they are tied to our values and assumptions about aging.

Perspective is important. The perspective that is chosen has implications for the questions that are asked, the interpretations that are made, and the policies that are recommended. Because perspective is so closely tied to values, there is no one "right" perspective. Given the importance of perspective and the number of competing perspectives on aging, it is necessary for us to examine the dominant ones. This examination will allow us to evaluate and analyse the literature on women and aging in a more informed way.

PSYCHOLOGICAL PERSPECTIVES ON ADULT DEVELOPMENT

The study of adult development is a component of developmental psychology which is concerned with individual development over time. Traditionally, attention to individual change has focussed upon childhood and adolescence when change is most visible and rapid. The assumption of many early developmental theorists, such as Freud and Piaget, was that development has an endpoint, *i.e.*, it is completed sometime in late adolescence or early adulthood after which a long period of stability ensues. The period of maturity is followed by one of degeneration in late adulthood. More recently psychologists have moved away from this view and have begun to examine adulthood and old age as periods of continuing growth, change, and development.

However, certain problems that are less apparent when studying young children become critical in studying change in adults. One major issue is that change does not occur as rapidly or as dramatically in adults. Often changes we may be interested in, such as growth in self-esteem or the development of identity as a professional, may occur over decades. At the same time that the individual is changing, the society she[2] lives in is also changing, often in ways that interact with her own individual change. For example, the greater proportions of women entering the paid labour force in Canada in the past decades (Armstrong 1984) and the parallel change in attitudes that has accompanied this major social change may significantly influence the way in which an individual woman develops her identity as a worker.

There are basically three perspectives on human development that developmental theorists have used. Although we will discuss each of these separately, it is important to remember that there is, in the minds of most psychologists, an overlap among various aspects of these perspectives.

The Mechanistic Perspective

The mechanistic perspective views change as the result of external forces (reinforcements and punishments) which act on individuals. The assumptions here include: (1) human beings operate in a manner analogous to machines; (2) all behaviour can be reduced to its components; (3) the organism or human being is *reactive*, that is, the individual does not initiate behaviour but rather reacts to events in the external environment; (4) all change is quantitative and continuous; (5) the organism is an open system and there is no endpoint to development; and (6) behaviour can be explained by basic laws. There is no assumption that development yields universal results. Rather, the focus is on how an individual's behaviour relates to the situation she is in. Because behaviour is situationally specific, the mechanistic perspective denies any kind of internal consistency to people's behaviour.

While few adult development theorists have adopted a mechanistic perspective in their work, it is important to include it in our discussion for comparative purposes and because it is the basis of much empirical work. One exception is Ahammer (1973) who, using social learning theory, argues that socialization in adulthood occurs because we reinforce, and are reinforced by others, in ways that demand change.

The Organismic Perspective

In contrast to the mechanistic perspective, the organismic perspective emphasizes the role of internal factors or forces in individual change. Thus, most of the assumptions of the organismic perspective are opposite to those of the mechanistic perspective. These assumptions include: (1) behaviour cannot be reduced to simple components or, in other words, the whole is greater than the sum of the parts; (2) while change can be either qualitative or quantitative, the more interesting changes are qualitative; (3) the organism or individual is *active*, not reactive, and acts on the environment to change it; (4) the cause of change is internal and involves a re-organization of the individual's cognitive and emotional structures; (5) human behaviour is governed by unique and complex principles that cannot be reduced to simple laws applicable to all organisms — again the whole is greater than the sum of the parts; and (6) the organism is a closed system which means there is an endpoint or goal to development.

Theories based on the organismic perspective look to the individual for the causes of change. It is assumed that development involves changes in, and usually increasingly complex organizations of, internal structures. These structures represent how we think about the world (Piaget 1983), and how we build relationships with other people (Erikson 1980a; 1980b; 1982). Also characteristic of the organismic perspective is an assumption that development takes place through a series of quantitative changes called stages. Stage theories postulate a universal series of stages, that is, all people develop by proceeding through these stages. Stages are usually seen to be invariant in sequence; that is, one must experience stage two before it is possible to experience stage three. Each stage builds and depends on the previous stage but, at the same time, is logically and quantitatively different from the preceding stage. Each stage represents the integration of a large amount of information from a wide range of experiences and is thus not limited to a specific context or content. The change from one state to the next is determined by internal factors, not external events. External events may speed up or slow down an individual's progress through the stage sequence, but they will not alter the order or the nature of the change which occurs. The most well-known theory of adult development based on an organismic perspective is Erikson's (1980a; 1980b; 1982) stage theory. Erikson postulates eight stages in his life-span developmental theory, the last three of which occur during adulthood.

The Dialectical Perspective

The third perspective shares some of the assumptions of the other two, focussing upon an integration of both external and internal forces as causes of change. The assumptions of the dialectical model are: (1) the individual is *both* active and reactive, that is, she both initiates change in her world and responds to demands that are placed on her; (2) change occurs as a result of conflict which may be internal, external, or a combination of both; (3) while both quantitative and qualitative change are possible, the focus is on qualitative change which results when a conflict is solved and a new synthesis formed; (4) the organism is an open system, that is, there is no endpoint or goal to development and as long as there is conflict and the person is able to perceive and respond to it, development is possible; and (5) historical change, in the form of large social movements or important events such as wars, depressions, entering the space age, and the development of television, is assumed to be important in influencing individual change.

The most important assumption of the dialectical model for adult development is the emphasis on historical change. Historical change as a factor influencing individual change is particularly relevant in adult development as change takes place over long periods of time. Also, adults are aware of, and involved in, the larger social world to a degree that children are not. While economic recession may indirectly affect children through their parents, it is the adult worker who must face unemployment, reduced income, and the worries of not being able to provide for her family.

The dialectical perspective posits an active changing individual in an active changing world. Interactions between the individual and the world, and particularly conflicts between the two, are the basis of developmental change. Both conflict and resolution (change) are important. In contrast, the mechanistic and organismic perspectives assume that stability or resolution is the desired state; conflict is only the means to the end. The dialectical perspective emphasizes the desire to engage in conflict as much as the desire to seek resolution. Conflict is important because it motivates the person to seek resolution, and resolution is important because it motivates the person to engage in more complex conflicts. Riegel (1975) describes the dialectical perspective as the "psychology of excitement" in contrast to the other perspectives which represent the "psychology of satisfaction."

The dialectical perspective has not been used in the establishment of major theories of adult development, but has been extremely influential in the interpretation of research. In particular, the emphasis on historical change has resulted in important reinterpretations of data. One example is the study of intellectual changes with age. A number of studies has tested young and old adults on standardized intelligence tests. The usual findings, that older people do less well than younger people, were long assumed to represent a decline in intelligence with age. However, if one examines the educational level of the two groups, the younger people are found to have more years of formal education. Since the 1890s, each succeeding generation has been more highly educated. Furthermore, it is well established that intelligence as measured by IQ tests is highly related to years of formal education. Thus, any study comparing younger people and older people is likely to find that older people do less well on IQ tests. This result may very well be due, not to a change in intelligence as people age, but to the higher educational level of the younger group. This example is particularly applicable to women, given that educational gains among women have been striking in the last few decases.

SOCIOLOGICAL PERSPECTIVES ON AGING

Unlike the situation in psychology, in which the study of human development has only recently turned its attention to issues related to later adulthood, within the sociology of aging the original focus was on old people. Indeed, for many years, the sociology of aging was the sociology of the aged. Only recently has the sociology of aging broadened its subject matter to encompass younger age groups and the entire life-course.[3]

Another area of contrast between sociology and psychology in terms of the topic of aging lies in the focussing of inquiry. Within psychology, the area of inquiry is delimited, with a narrow focus on adult development, and stability and change therein. The sociology of aging, on the other hand, deals with a much more amorphous subject matter,[4] ranging from individual adjustment to old age, at the micro-level, to such macro-level concerns as the dynamics of population aging and the role of age as a structural component of society.

Within sociology as a whole, and the sociology of aging, it is customary to distinguish between micro and macro-levels of analysis. The micro-level focusses upon issues relating to the individual and to the social interactions in which individuals are engaged; the macro-level is concerned with the structural components of society and their interrelationships. In reality, of course, there is no clear-cut distinction between the micro and macro social worlds. The behaviour and social interactions of individuals are influenced by the wider social structure: society as a whole is influenced by the actions of individuals. Nevertheless, the distinction is maintained for analytical reasons — as a tool to guide theory formation and empirical research.

Within sociology, two competing theoretical perspectives exist, the normative perspective and the interpretive perspective. We will discuss each briefly, in terms of their assumptions about society and the individual in society. Within each perspective, both micro and macro issues can be, and are, addressed. It should be noted that the distinction between normative and interpretive perspectives will be somewhat over-simplified for illustrative purposes. In reality, there is somewhat more overlap and agreement than is presented here.

The Normative Perspective

The normative perspective focusses upon social order, which is viewed as desirable, and the mechanisms of social control that are created to maintain order. Individuals behave in "orderly" or conforming ways due to their socialization, and internalization, of society's norms (rules) and values. Society's norms and values are external to the individual; they are imposed upon her and she conforms to them in robot-like fashion. It will be noted that this perspective shares at least one assumption with the mechanistic perspective discussed earlier, namely, that the individual is reactive to the wider environment.

A major example of the normative perspective is structural-functionalism. Once the dominant theoretical perspective within American sociology, it continues to be influential, although its popularity has waned in recent years. The structural-functionalist position rests on a number of assumptions about society and individuals: (1) cooperation is a basic characteristic of social life; (2) the different parts of society (institutions, organizations, and groups) exist in an interdependent relationship with one another through processes of exchange and reciprocity; (3) society is held together by shared values; (4) societies, like biological organisms, seek to maintain homeostasis, or a "natural" equilibrium; and (5) individual behaviour is determined and regulated by societal rules.

Within the sociology of aging, a number of theories have been informed with a structural-functionalist perspective, most notably age-stratification theory (Riley *et al.* 1972), a macro-theory, and disengagement theory[5] (Cumming and Henry 1961), a micro-theory. Although differing in many ways, these two theories share a focus on role allocation based on age, and view the loss of roles in later life (particularly the work role) as important for the maintenance of the equilibrium of the wider society.

The Interpretive Perspective

The interpretive perspective embodies two divergent sets of theoretical formulations which generally correspond to the micro-macro distinction made above. At the macro-level, the conflict perspective (encompassing Marxist, neo-Marxist, and critical theory) is dominant. Its assumptions, generally opposite to those of structural-functionalism, include: (1) conflict is a basic characteristic of social life; (2) the different parts of society exist in relations of exploitation; (3) there are no shared values in society — the dominant values in society are those of the politically dominant group; (4) society is held together by the powerful, who possess the resources to demand compliance, in both overt and subtle ways; and (5) change, not homeostatis (or equilibrium), is the "natural" state of society. It will be noted that the conflict perspective shares with the dialectical perspective a focus on conflict as a basic characteristic of social life.

While the conflict perspective has a long history within sociology as a whole, only in recent years has it emerged within the sociology of aging. Marshall (1980, 116) refers to this development as the "new political sociology of aging," and a leading Canadian proponent of this perspective is Myles (1984). It focusses upon such issues as the causes of poverty among the elderly population, the role of values (ideology) in legitimizing age-related poverty, and the role of pension funds as a source of capital (power) for governments and corporations.

At the micro-level, the interpretive perspective embodies a number of assumptions about individuals in social life. In contrast to the normative perspective with its view of the individual as a willing and compliant rule-follower, the interpretive perspective holds that individuals are active *creators* of the social order. Individuals engage in social interactions to which they bring their *own* definitions, meanings, and interpetations. Individuals are not controlled by society; rather, individuals create their own meaning in life and can change society through social interactions. The assumption that individuals create their own reality is similar to the assumption of an active individual within the organismic perspective.

Symbolic interactionism and social exchange are two theories within the interpretive perspective that have been used quite widely within the sociology of aging. Symbolic interactionism focusses primarily on how older individuals interpret and give meaning to events and situations in their lives, *e.g.*, residence in nursing homes and age-segregated housing, terminal illness and societal definitions of uselessness. Social exchange theory, in a somewhat different vein, looks at how older people deal with diminished resources in their exchange relationships with other people.

THE POLICY IMPLICATIONS OF PERSPECTIVE

It is important to realize that the perspective or perspectives we use to examine women and aging are important not only for theory development and the interpretation of data, but also in the formation of political views and social policy. In turn, our political views lead us to favour some perspectives over others. While it is true that, as taught in introductory psychology and sociology courses, social science research strives to be as objective as possible, in actual fact our values and assumptions about the world are always intertwined with our observations.

The mechanistic perspective, with its emphasis on the external determinants of behaviour, favours an interventionist approach. If one assumes that people behave in ways determined by the situation they find themselves in, then one examines and changes situations in order to achieve certain goals. For example, studies (Rodin 1983; Schulz 1980; Schulz and Brenner 1977) have shown old people in nursing homes have better physical health, life satisfaction, and activity level if they perceive that they have control over their environment than if they perceive that they have no control. Knowing this, nursing homes and government policy regulating nursing homes can change the environment in ways to increase people's perceived and actual control.

The organismic perspective, on the other hand, encourages a more conservative approach. If there is a universal series of stages that people go through, if the order is invariant, and if the motivation for change is internal, outside intervention will be ineffective. Further, these assumptions do not lead the researcher or the policy-maker to examine larger historical and social factors, such as gender,[6] that may be important as people age. Growing old and female may be very different from growing old and male.

The dialectical perspective, with its emphasis on both external and internal forces as well as historical change, allows for the most complex views of aging individuals and social policy. Given the emphasis on historical change, one can assume that the needs of elderly persons are not constant across generations, but vary with the experiences and life styles of the people involved. Thus, a generation of women who had large families and did not participate in large numbers in the labour force had different needs than a generation of women who has few children and participates in the labour force most of their lives. The first group is more likely to live with kin, especially daughters, when elderly, and pensions for housewives is a critical policy issue for them. For the latter group of women, alternate housing is critical, as well as changes in labour-force-related pensions.

The normative perspective provides contradictory implications for policy-makers. On the one hand, its complacent assumptions about the existing status quo suggest a non-interventionist approach. Our treatment of the elderly is functional for the maintenance of societal equilibrium. Given that societal equilibrium is viewed as a highly desirable goal, we should not do anything to upset it. On the other hand, there is recognition that societies do change, particularly within age stratification theory. And, as societies change, there is a need to respond to that change, e.g., alter existing age-related rules. Thus, given the increase in the proportion of our population that is aged, and expectations concerning future increases, it is functional for societal stability to revise pension and retirement policies. In other words, the desired end (stability) may only be accomplished through means which entail change.

The interpretive perspective (at the macro-level) has clear implications for the wider society, although not ones that may be popular with Canadian policy-makers. Corporate capitalism is responsible for the devalued social and economic position of elderly people. A radical restructuring of the existing economic and political system is needed to fundamentally alter the lives of old people.

The interpretive perspective (at the micro-level) has quite a different set of policy implications. Here the view of individuals is one of active creators of the social order. This points towards a scenario in which social policy changes occur as a direct response to the actions of older people. On the other hand, its focus on the extent to which individuals are able to manage on their own, through their definitions and interpretations of situations and events, suggests a conservative, non-interventionist policy approach.

THE STUDY OF WOMEN AND AGING

None of the perspectives we have discussed were designed with women in mind or based on women's experiences. While this does not mean we can or should brush them aside, it does raise the question of their applicability to the topic of women and aging. Our opinion is that all of these perspectives *can* be applied to the study of women as they age. Indeed, most have been, either explicitly or implicitly. The questions that they raise are general ones, that can be applied to either women or men. This, however, does not preclude the possibility that the answers will differ for women and men. For example, a stage theory (organismic perspective) may be applied to either sex, but the stages experienced by women may differ from those of men. Indeed, Erickson's stage theory has been criticized for being more applicable to men's lives than to women's lives (Gilligan 1982; Rossi 1980). The perspective itself may apply to both women and men, but the details of the stages may be gender-specific. Another example is the conflict perspective within sociology. The poverty of both women and men in later life can be fruitfully examined using this perspective, but the factors contributing to that poverty may differ for women as compared to men.

In recent years, a call for a feminist perspective on aging has emerged (*e.g.*, Burwell 1984; Cohen 1984; Nett 1982). A feminist perspective begins with the idea that the status and position of older women is not universal, but varies with the wider social, economic, and cultural context. In contemporary society, older women are devalued and powerless as a direct result of a wider society that oppresses all women, regardless of age, in the interests of preserving a male-dominated social order. The low status of older women represents an extension and intensification of the negative impact of sexist society, due to the added factors of age stigmatization and physical frailty. Indeed, Nett (1982) argues that the low status of old people in general results from the fact that so many old people are women. According to this argument, ageism is a byproduct of sexism.

Central to the feminist perspective is the proposition that the lack of power and status characteristic of older women results from the limited options open to them earlier in their lives. Societal definitions of what woman can do and be are more narrow than is the case for men. It is not so much that men and women "march to different drummers" as it is that "they are not even in the same parade" (Mackie 1986, 100). Women are supposed to *be* attractive to men and to *do* work for men (and their children). Then, as women age, losing their attractiveness and becoming widows, their social usefulness is gone. Even women who do not meet societal expectations, either by choice or chance, cannot avoid negative evaluation — they are "failures" as women. In other words, both success and failure at being a woman results, inevitably, in what sociologists term a "spoiled" identity.

It is obvious, then, that feminists view the problems that older women face as being socially imposed. As Nett (1982, 225) puts it: "As elders we are too wise to look inward any more to find the reason for our oppression" and "as feminists ... we have had considerable practice in refusing to accept the blame for our victimization." Therefore, change in societal attitudes and practices are required to raise the status of older women.

We agree that a feministic perspective on women and aging is valuable in examining the situation of women as they age, and we incorporate it throughout this monograph. However, we will not limit ourselves to this perspective because we do not want to exclude the insights that are provided by other perspectives. By using a range of perspectives, our aim is to provide an overview of the literature on women and aging that is as comprehensive and accurate as possible.

It should be pointed out that a considerable amount of the research concerned with women and aging is based on no explicit, general, theoretical perspective. Rather it is *issue-related, descriptive* work. While this may partially be a function of the fact that the study of women and aging is quite new, we feel that another factor is operating as well. The general failure to incorporate women into mainstream theoretical perspectives on aging is a reflection of our resistance to incorporate women into society and, hence, into sociological and psychological research. Social science research is not value-free: the questions that are asked and the way they are studied reflect the cultural and social context in which researchers live. As we live in a society in which women play a peripheral role (except in the home), it is not surprising that women have been understudied in a way that mirrors their marginality.

The specific topics chosen for study also reflect our cultural biases concerning the "proper" sphere for women. As pointed out by Barnett and Baruch (1978), a central focus of inquiry has been on women's reproductive and familial roles, *e.g.*, menopause, "empty nest," widowhood adjustment. Less attention has been paid to women's roles outside the home *e.g.*, work in the labour force or in voluntary associations. While we will not ignore the "traditional" topics, we make every effort to present women's aging in a broader way, incorporating discussions of less well-studied aspects of women's lives and changes with age.

METHODOLOGICAL ISSUES

Research Designs

In order to study aging, one must observe, question, or test different individuals at different time periods. That is, we must in some way measure what we are interested in, and then examine how this behaviour changes over time. There are several ways to do this, and no research design is without its problems. We will now look at various research designs and examine their benefits and drawbacks.

In the *cross-sectional design*, different groups of people are studied at the same time. For example, a group of 20 year-olds, another group of 40 year-olds, and a third group of 60 year-olds are given the same questionnaire or test, and comparisons are made. The cross-sectional design is very common; the large majority of studies on aging uses a cross-sectional design. Of the studies discussed in this book, most employ this design.

Despite its popularity, there are some problems with the cross-sectional design. If the age groups studied do not respond similarly, the researcher has observed an *age difference*. This age difference can be explained in one of two ways. It is possible that what is observed is an *age change*. That is, the differences observed are due to maturational or experiential factors that change with chronological age. Often age differences in cross-sectional studies are interpreted as age changes. However, there is another, equally likely, possibility: the observed age differences are due to *cohort differences*. A cohort is a group of people born at the same time. A cohort might, for example, be defined as all people born between 1940 and 1949, or all people born in 1930. If the different cohorts studied in a cross-sectional study vary on some factor which is related to their responses to the task, it may be that these cohort differences explain the different responses of the various age groups and that age changes are not involved at all.

It is crucial to remember that in any cross-sectional study, it is impossible to know which of these two explanations is more valid. One can logically try to eliminate one explanation (*e.g.*, by testing three different age groups with the same number of years of education), but one is never sure which explanation accounts for the difference. Age changes and cohort differences are always confounded (tied together with no certain way to untie them) in the cross-sectional research design.

Since most of the research on women and aging is cross-sectional, confounding of age changes and cohort differences is an ever-present problem that must be considered when evaluating research. In reviewing many areas of research for this book (*e.g.*, women's health-care patterns, women's participation in the workforce and their attitudes towards employment and retirement, sexual behaviour, and attitudes and patterns of family interaction), we have been aware of the problems inherent in assuming age change from cross-sectional studies and encourage the reader to pay special attention to these problems.

In the *longitudinal design*, one age cohort is studied at different ages. For example, a group of 20 year-olds is studied three times — once in 1985 when they are aged 20, again in 1995 when they are aged 30, and a third time in 2005 when they are aged 40. Each time they are given the same tests or questionnaires. The longitudinal design has several advantages over the cross-sectional design. Since the same people are followed over time, one knows that the changes are not due to cohort differences as long as more than one cohort is included in the study. Also the longitudinal design allows an examination of intra-individual change since the same people are tested over time.

However, there are several disadvantages inherent to the longitudinal design. It takes a much longer time to complete because one must wait for respondents to age. It is usually more expensive than the cross-sectional design. The researcher must also be concerned about such issues as "practice effects" (do people change their responses as a function of experience with the study?) and "experimental mortality" effects (are the people who do not return for the second or third testing different from those who remain?).

In addition to these problems, the longitudinal study suffers from a confounding effect, although in a slightly different way from the cross-sectional design. As with the cross-sectional study, the researcher has observed age differences, and there are two possible explanations for these differences. The first possibility is that the differences represent an *age change*. That is, as people become older, they may change in ways that are reflected on the measurement used. The second explanation is that the differences may be due to *time of measurement* differences. That is, over the period of study there may have been general cultural changes which influence all peoples' responses in the same way and if another age group had been studied it would have shown similar changes over the same time period.

Although many fewer studies are longitudinal, it is important to be aware of these confounding effects. This is particularly true when studying women and aging, because recent historical changes in attitudes toward women and in women's behaviours and roles have been so pervasive and received so much media attention that any longitudinal study involving a single cohort of women must consider the effects of historical change as a possible explanation of observed age differences.

In an attempt to overcome some of the problems associated with cross-sectional and longitudinal designs, some researchers (*e.g.*, Schaie 1973; 1977) have recommended *sequential designs*. These designs employ a series of cross-sectional or a series of longitudinal studies. In the cross-sectional sequential design, several cross-sectional studies are carried out at different times. In the longitudinal-sequential design, several different cohorts are studied over the same age range.

Sequential designs are very useful in separating age changes from historical changes. As an example, let us look at a recent longitudinal-sequential study. Doherty and Baldwin (1985) examine changes in locus of control for a young and middle-aged cohort of women and men at three different time periods — late 1960s, early 1970s, and mid-1970s. Locus of control was measured by a series of questions designed to explore the extent to which people perceive that events are under their own (internal) control versus under the control of others (external). The researchers found no changes over the three measurement times among the male respondents in either cohort. Among the women, both cohorts became significantly more external from the second testing (early 1970s) to the third testing (mid-1970s). Given that the difference in locus of control occurred only for women, and given that it occurred for two different cohorts of women, the authors conclude that the change in women's attitudes was a result of the feminist movement. This movement became much more prominent in the early to mid-1970s and emphasized discrimination and other unfair practices which were imposed on women from the outside. This is interpretation, not fact, and neither the authors nor anyone else can know for sure what really caused the pattern of results. However, because two cohorts were followed rather than just one, and because the same pattern of results occurred for both cohorts, the authors' explanation of historical, rather than age, change is strengthened.

Research Issues Related to the Study of Women and Aging

The problems inherent in the research designs just discussed are "gender-blind." In other words, regardless of whether women, men, or both, are studied, the same problems exist. However, there are a number of methodological issues relevant to the study of women and aging only. We will now address these issues briefly.

First, while we do not completely agree with the argument that women have been neglected in the study of aging (*e.g.*, Burwell 1984; Cohen 1984), there has been a tendency, as we mentioned previously, to focus on topics that reinforce stereotypes about women and to neglect other important research subjects. Also, there has been a tendency in the literature to make generalizations from male samples to the total (male and female) population (Burwell 1984). This practice makes the assumption that male behaviour is the "norm" and diverts our attention away from gender differences in aging and the unique aspects of aging for women. In this monograph, we examine research findings that pertain to women only, to differences between women and men, or to documented similarities between women and men.

Second, most of the studies on women and aging have treated "women" as if they were a homogeneous group. Our original intention was to include a chapter on variations among women in terms of the sociological and psychological aspects of aging. However, this proved to be impossible due to a paucity of research focussing upon such variation. Particularly disappointing was the lack of information on class and ethnic differences in the aging experience of women. While we cannot rectify this situation, we make every attempt to include information on women with different psychological and sociological characteristics. At present, we can only emphasize the importance of an approach to our topic that recognizes the heterogeneity of the aging experience for women; that recognizes that "women" are not all alike in either objective or subjective ways, just as "old people" display significant variations in life situations and personal orientation.

Last, it has been argued (Burwell 1984) that the choice of methods used in the study of women and aging tends to contain a male bias. It is possible that more naturalistic and qualitative methodologies (sometimes viewed as "second class" methodologies by "real" scientists) are appropriate to the study of women and aging, given that women may define their social world in a way that emphasizes the quality of interpersonal relationships — a dimension that tends to be overlooked in more rigorous, quantitative studies.

NOTES

1. Following McPherson (1983), we define perspective as a general view of a phenomenon; a global term referring to groups of theories sharing underlying premises and a general orientation. A theory, on the other hand, is a specific explanation of a phenomenon.
2. Since the subject of this book is women, we have chosen to use she as the generic pronoun.
3. This is not to say that young people have been ignored by sociologists in general. There has been a long-standing interest within sociology in topics related to children and young people (*e.g.*, socialization, juvenile delinquency). However, this work is quite separate from that which is considered to fall under the "sociology of aging" rubric.
4. Given the diversity of perspectives and theories within the sociology of aging, we will discuss only those that have relevance for later issues in this monograph. For a comprehensive overview of sociological perspectives and theories, see Binstock and Shanas (1985), Marshall (1980), and McPherson (1983).
5. It is interesting to note that disengagement theory may be viewed as representative of the normative perspective within sociology, given its equilibrium assumptions, as well as the organismic perspective within psychology, given its assumption concerning internally generated voluntary withdrawal from social roles.
6. Our usage of the terms gender and sex requires clarification. Gender refers to differences between females and males that are socially defined and socially constructed. Therefore, gender varies across societies and

over time, as societies change. Sex refers to differences that are physiologically based, *e.g.*, the fact that women can bear children and men cannot is a sex difference. In reference to differences that have both a biological and a social component (*e.g.*, differences between females and males in life expectancy), we use the term sex. Also, the term sex is used to refer to characteristics that have no behavioural connotation. For example, the relative proportion of males and females in a population is the sex structure (or sex composition) of that population.

CHAPTER 2

THE DEMOGRAPHIC BACKGROUND: AGING IS A WOMEN'S ISSUE

THE CANADIAN AGE-SEX STRUCTURE — 1941, 1981, 2021

It is a well-established fact that the Canadian population is "aging," with aging defined as a trend of increase in the proportion of the total population that is aged 65 and over.[1] Population aging has been occurring throughout most of this century, but the rate has accelerated in recent decades and is expected to increase substantially in future decades. For example, the percentage of the total population aged 65 and over was approximately 5 percent at the turn of the century, 6.7 percent in 1941, 9.7 percent in 1981, and is expected to exceed 19 percent by 2021.[2]

The major factor accounting for this increase in the percentage of older people is declining fertility. In other words, increases in the proportion of older people in our population are a direct result of decreases in the proportion of children. Contrary to popular opinion, declining mortality plays a *minor* role in altering the age structure of a population. Simply put, our population is *not* aging because we are living longer; our population *is* aging because we are producing many fewer babies per woman. If we were to experience a major upswing in fertility (which most demographers consider unlikely), our population would stop aging even if mortality remained unchanged or improved. Further information on the causes of demographic aging can be obtained from McDaniel's (1986) book, *Canada's Aging Population*.

In conjuction with these changes in the age structure, significant changes in the sex structure have also occurred. As our population ages, an increasingly larger percentage of the population is composed of women. Table 2.1 presents data on the relative numbers of males and females in Canada, by ten-year age groups, for 1941 and 1981, and provides projected estimates for 2021. The sex ratios[3] in the table indicate the degree to which the Canadian population is becoming dominated by women, numerically speaking. In 1941, there were 105 males for every 100 females (all ages combined). By 1981, the sex ratio had declined to 98 males per 100 females, and a further decline to about 97 is expected by 2021.

TABLE 2.1

POPULATION BY SEX AND AGE GROUPS (IN THOUSANDS), AND SEX RATIOS, CANADA: 1941, 1981, 2021

	1941[a]			1981			2021		
	Males	Females	SR[b]	Males	Females	SR	Males	Females	SR
Age									
0–9	1,063.0	1,034.7	103	1,827.5	1,733.8	105	1,636.3	1,552.4	105
10–19	1,121.5	1,099.4	102	2,166.7	2,069.0	105	1,664.9	1,581.7	104
20–29	1,006.3	993.2	101	2,258.7	2,262.7	100	1,833.6	1,758.3	104
30–39	828.1	775.4	107	1,843.8	1,825.1	101	2,025.6	1,952.1	104
40–49	681.1	630.5	108	1,309.4	1,283.8	102	1,897.0	1,854.1	102
50–59	591.1	507.4	116	1,190.1	1,233.3	96	2,094.4	2,119.1	99
60–69	381.1	333.8	114	853.0	970.7	88	1,934.2	2,135.7	91
70–79	178.4	174.5	102	461.7	604.4	76	1,212.8	1,464.9	83
80–89	46.7	52.4	89	138.9	248.8	56	407.8	673.4	61
90+	3.3	4.8	69	19.6	43.2	45	54.7	167.5	33
All ages	5,900.6	5,606.1	105	12,069.4	12,274.8	98	14,761.3	15,259.2	97

[a] Excludes Newfoundland

[b] SR = sex ratio = number of males per 100 females

SOURCES: *1961 Census of Canada*, Catalogue No. 92-542, Table 20; *1981 Census of Canada*, Catalogue No. 92-901, Table 1; Statistics Canada, *Population Projections for Canada, Provinces and Territories*, Catalogue No. 91-520, 1985.

However, more important is the way that sex ratios vary by age. It is clear from Table 2.1 that young age groups are male-dominated and old age groups are female-dominated, and increasingly so with advancing age. This pattern appears for all three years (1941, 1981, 2021), but the trend becomes more pronounced over time, in two ways. First, the "cut-off" age at which women outnumber men has become younger. In 1941, female numerical dominance does not become manifest until the age group 80–89 while, in both 1981 and 2021, women outnumber men at all age groups after 50–59. Second, the degree of female "excess" at older ages increases over time. Focussing on the ages 90 and over, the sex ratio declined from 69 in 1941 to 45 in 1981 and is expected to decrease further to 33 by 2021.

It is clear, then, that the elderly female population has increased, and is expected to increase in the future, at a faster rate than the elderly male population. While the population aged 65 and over for both sexes has grown at a rate far surpassing that of the total population for the period 1941–1981, and the same trend is expected for the period 1981–2021, the increase in the very old female population relative to the increase in the very old male population is substantial. As shown in Table 2.2, for the period 1941–1981, the female population aged 90 and over increased by 800 percent

TABLE 2.2

PERCENTAGE INCREASE IN THE ELDERLY POPULATION, BY SEX, CANADA: 1941–81, 1981–2021

Age	Increase (%)			
	1941–1981 (Actual)		1981–2021 (Projected)	
	Female	Male	Female	Male
65–69	212.5	140.4	120.7	127.3
70–74	232.3	152.9	143.7	160.3
75–79	268.2	168.6	140.6	166.3
80–84	332.9	178.3	152.2	190.3
85–89	479.0	249.2	204.5	200.6
90 +	800.0	493.9	287.7	179.1
All ages (0–90 +)	119.0	104.5	24.3	22.4

SOURCE: as in Table 2.1.

whereas the comparable male population increased by a smaller amount, 493.9 percent. A similar trend is projected for the period 1981–2021, although the magnitude of the differential increase is expected to be smaller — a 287.7 percent increase for women compared to 179.1 percent increase for men.

As the trends depicted in Tables 2.1 and 2.2 show, the elderly population is becoming increasingly "female-loaded," particularly the population at very advanced ages.[4] Let us now turn to some factors that may account for these trends.

FACTORS ACCOUNTING FOR THE CHANGING SEX STRUCTURE

As already stated, the major determinant of population aging is declining fertility. However, the changing sex structure (or sex composition) of our population that has occurred in conjunction with our changing age structure is due to an entirely different set of factors. Sex structure is altered by two demographic processes: migration, which generally plays a small role; and mortality, which is the major determinant.

Migration

Migration plays a role in affecting sex structure only when migrants are more likely to be of one sex than the other. If approximately equal numbers of males and females migrate, the sex composition in both the "receiver" country and the "sender" country is not affected. Historically, Canada has been a "receiver" country and migration has been "sex selective" in favour of males, *i.e.*, more males than females migrated to Canada. This pattern was likely a result of the greater freedom given to men to travel the distances required for international migration. Also, for some periods in our history, men only were recruited to fill specific labour needs, *e.g.*, as when Chinese men were brought into Canada to build the railway through the western provinces. In addition, western cultural expectations that men be the primary economic supporters provided a motivation for them to migrate to areas perceived to offer economic opportunities.

The effects of this sex selectivity can be seen in the data presented in Table 2.1 for 1941. Large sex ratios in favour of males are evident, especially for the ages from 50 through to 69. They are the result of the large numbers of young men that immigrated to Canada in the early decades of this century. Indeed, through most of our history, Canadian society has contained more men than women due to this migration factor.

However, by the 1980s, this traditional pattern of over-representation of males in international migration flows to Canada has ceased. Indeed, in recent years, there have been slightly more female than male migrants to Canada; approximately 96 male immigrants for every 100 female immigrants. If this trend continues, the role of migration in influencing the Canadian sex structure will be reversed. However, the magnitude of female numerical dominance in migration at the current time is small compared to that of male dominance in the past. Therefore, assuming that a large influx of female immigrants does not occur (and there is no reason for expecting such a trend), the future role of international migration in Canada will be one of making a slight contribution to increasing the number of females relative to males in our population.

Mortality

Mortality is the major factor accounting for our changing sex structure. This is so because Canadian females have a substantially greater life expectancy than Canadian males: at the present time, the difference in life expectancy at birth is approximately seven years in favour of females. Throughout the course of this century, the female longevity advantage has been steadily increasing. As shown in Figure 2.1, the sex difference in life expectancy at birth in 1931 (the earliest census year for which reliable data are available) was only about two years. At that time, females could expect to live 62.1 years, and males, 60.0 years. As life expectancy at birth has steadily increased to the present 79.0 years for females, and 71.9 years for males, the gap between female and male longevity has substantially widened.

Critical to an aging population is the degree to which female life expec-

FIGURE 2.1

LIFE EXPECTANCY AT BIRTH AND AT AGE 65, BY SEX, CANADA: 1931 — 1980-82

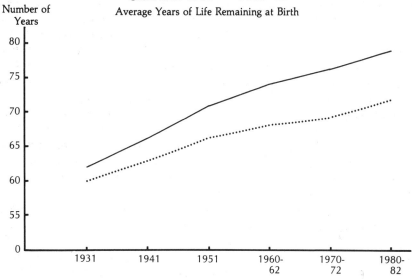

Number of Years

Average Years of Life Remaining at Birth

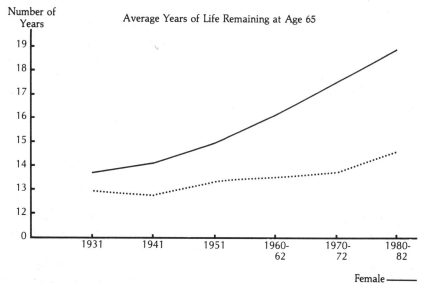

Number of Years

Average Years of Life Remaining at Age 65

Female ——————
Male ············

SOURCES: *Life Tables for Canada and Regions, 1931 and 1941*, D.B.S. Catalogue No. 48-515; *Canadian Life Tables, 1951*, D.B.S. Catalogue No. 84-509; *Canadian Life Tables, 1960-62*, D.B.S. Catalogue No. 84-516; *Life Tables, Canada and Provinces, 1970-1972* and *Life Tables, Canada and Provinces, 1980-1982*, Statistics Canada Catalogue No. 84-532.

tancy gains at the older ages have exceeded male life expectancy gains. Figure 2.1 also presents data on expected years of life remaining at age 65 for women and men for the period from 1931 to 1980–82. It is readily apparent that 65 year-old women have made large gains in life expectancy (5.1 years) relative to 65 year-old men (1.6 years) in the past 50 years. Indeed, for females, *30 percent* of additional life attained since 1931 results from gains in life expectancy after age 65, whereas for males, the comparable figure is only *13 percent*.

This information helps to clarify the data presented earlier in Table 2.2. The substantially larger percentage increase in the older female population compared to the older male population (for the period 1941–1981) is the direct result of these sex differences in mortality. Given the significance of sex mortality differentials in accounting for our changing sex structure, let us now turn our attention to possible explanations of why women live longer than men in Canada.

EXPLANATIONS OF SEX MORTALITY DIFFERENTIALS

Although it is commonly thought that the mortality advantage experienced by women is, and has always been, a universal phenomenon, there are reasons to doubt this proposition. Evidence from skeletal remains of populations existing in times pre-dating record keeping suggest a mortality advantage favouring males (Heligman 1983). In addition, in some underdeveloped countries, it has been found that girls and women experience higher death rates than their males counterparts (Lopez and Ruzicka 1983). Such findings have led to a conclusion that in high mortality environments, male life expectancy may exceed female life expectancy by three to four years (Ruzicka and Lado 1983), presumably as a result of high risks associated with childbearing and comparatively poorer nutrition for females, given their low social status. However, as societies undergo social and economic development, experiencing demographic transition (reduction in birth and death rates) and epidemiological transition (change in the major causes of death, from communicable or infectious diseases to degenerative diseases), the female advantage in mortality invariably emerges.

There are two major hypotheses regarding greater female survivorship: one focusses on the biological, physiological, and genetic superiority of females (*e.g.*, Madigan 1957; Rasmuson 1971); the other relates higher female survival to social and environmental factors (*e.g.*, Enterline 1961; Graney 1979; Harrison 1978; Retherford 1975). While there is a general consensus that *both* sets of factors — biological and social — play a role in sex mortality differentials, there is considerable disagreement about their relative importance.

The Biological Hypothesis

The basic argument in support of the biological hypothesis relates to the chromosomal difference between males and females. It is well known that females have an XX sex chromosomal structure whereas males have an XY structure, and that the Y chromosome is small and contains considerably less genetic information than the X chromosome. The possible survival advantages of the female genetic make-up are related to: (1) protection from X-linked recessive conditions; (2) greater fetal viability; (3) lower levels of infant mortality; (4) superior functioning of the immune system; and (5) female hormonal protection from heart disease. We will briefly examine findings relating to each of these issues.

Recent research from comparative biology indicates that the commonly held idea that greater female longevity is due to protection from X-linked recessive conditions cannot be empirically verified (Comfort 1979). While generalizations from non-humans to humans must always be made with caution, it has been found that females enjoy a mortality advantage even among biological groups in which males have a pair of like sex chromosomes. Further, it has been argued that, even if within humans some female survival advantage accrues from the genetic factor, it plays a small role in contributing to sex differences in mortality (Waldron 1983). This argument stresses that some X-linked recessive conditions are not fatal (*e.g.,* colour blindness) and others (*e.g.,* hemophilia) are very rare.

For many years, it has been asserted that males have much higher death rates *in utero* than females (McMillen 1979; Potts 1970; Rasmuson 1971). For example, Rasmuson (1971) estimates that the primary sex ratio (the sex ratio at conception) ranges from 120 to 150; McMillen (1979) states that a conservative estimate places the primary sex ratio at 120. As the sex ratio at birth approximates 105, these estimates are suggestive of heavy male fetal loss which could not be due to social or environmental factors, but rather results from the lower genetic viability of the male fetus. Up until very recently, high rates of male death *in utero* have been an accepted "fact," and have provided the basis for the strongest argument in favour of innate female superiority in survival. However, Waldron (1983) has attacked the accepted generalization of differential fetal mortality for females and males, and has garnered considerable evidence in support of her position that (a) we simply do not know, as yet, what sex differences in fetal mortality exist prior to the seventh month of gestation, due to methodological problems and inconsistent findings, and (b) for fetal mortality between the seventh and ninth months, males have higher fetal mortality in less developed societies whereas no consistent sex differences can be observed in more developed societies.

The evidence supportive of lower female infant mortality is quite consistent, on the other hand. Girl babies display substantially better survivorship in the first week of life and a smaller, yet important, advantage throughout the first year of life. The reasons for greater female survivorship in infancy are not established, but the differential itself (particularly in the first week of life) lends support to an inherent female biological viability in comparison to males.

It is generally found that females have lower death rates due to infectious diseases, particularly for the first year of life and for ages above 35 (Preston 1976). It has been confirmed that the X chromosome contains a number of genes which influence the functioning of the immune system (Waldron 1983). Therefore, it appears that the female genetic structure contributes to a greater resistance to infectious diseases.

Finally, in terms of the biological hypothesis, there is some evidence that lower rates of death due to ischaemic (coronary) heart disease for women are related to genetic factors. Specifically, it is argued that female sex hormones, particularly estrogen, decrease the risk of ischaemic heart disease (Waldron 1976). Also, there is recent evidence that indicates that estrogen protects against lung disorders (National Institutes of Health 1985).

The Social Hypothesis

The social hypothesis, while not denying the operation of genetic or biological factors in contributing to greater female longevity, either in themselves or in interaction with environmental factors, views the major determinants of sex mortality differentials as residing in the social and cultural environment. In particular, the existing system of gender roles is viewed as the important dimension of the social/cultural environment (*e.g.*, Graney 1979; Harrison 1978). The general argument is that males are socialized in ways that encourage behaviours that lower their survival chances. Such behaviours include: suppression of emotional expression; risk-taking actions that can result in accidental death; smoking and drinking as symbolic of "masculinity"; and aggressive and competitive "Type A" behaviour. In other words, the literature has tended to focus on what men "do wrong," rather than on what women "do right."

While males have higher mortality rates than females at all ages in Canada, the discussion of the social hypothesis can be facilitated by an examination of sex differences in death rates due to different causes of death. As shown in Table 2.3, the largest sex mortality differential occurs for suicide: males are nearly three and one-half times more likely to kill themselves than females. Higher rates of male suicide have been linked to male gender role behaviour in that the discouragement of self-disclosure, together with an emphasis on the pursuit of instrumental (or task-oriented) goals at the expense of emotional ones, may lead to high levels of stress, which may result in suicidal behaviour (Jourard 1974). However, it is

TABLE 2.3

DEATH RATES BY CAUSE AND SEX, AND SEX MORTALITY RATIOS: CANADA, 1983

Cause of Death	Male Rate (per 100,000 population)	Female Rate (per 100,000 population)	Sex Mortality Ratio[a]
Diseases of the Circulatory System	347.3	288.4	120
— Ischaemic Heart Disease	228.9	157.1	146
— Cerebrovascular Disease	49.5	63.5	78
Malignant Neoplasms	195.2	153.0	128
— of digestive organs	56.4	46.6	121
— of respiratory system	68.4	21.0	326
— of breast	—	30.4	—
— of genito-urinary system	29.3	22.1	133
Diseases of the Respiratory System	65.7	41.5	158
Acidents	51.6	22.7	227
— Motor Vehicle	25.6	9.4	272
— Other	26.0	13.3	195
Suicide	23.4	6.9	339

[a] Sex mortality ratio = male rate divided by female rate.

SOURCE: Computed from data in Statistics Canada, *Vital Statistics, 1983, Vol. 4, Causes of Death*, Catalogue No. 84-203.

important to note that suicide attempt rates are quite similar for females and males (Graney 1979), but that males are more "efficient." The greater cultural acceptability for females to seek help may result in females using suicide attempts as a "cry for help," whereas males use this option to a lesser extent. Or, it may be that the methods that women are more likely to use (*e.g.*, drug overdose) are easier to reverse.

Substantial sex differences in death rates due to accidents can also be observed in Table 2.3. Veevers and Gee (1986) suggest that gender roles can be related to differential fatal accident rates on a number of dimensions. First, the traditional division of labour between the sexes is such that women do less physically demanding, and hence, often less dangerous, tasks. This pattern, which can be observed in everyday behaviours such as driving a car and in household tasks whereby women do the "inside" work and men do the more hazardous "outside" work, appears to remain unchanged, despite recent changes in the role of women in modern society. Second, men and women vary in their recreational activities, a differential that can be observed as early as the elementary school ages (Lever 1976). Women tend toward leisure activities which are more likely to be indoors and which are more quiet and passive. Men are more likely to engage in vigorous outdoor activities which involve the possibility of danger and death, *e.g.*, contact sports, drag racing, mountain-climbing. While some women are beginning to be involved in comparable activities, their numbers are small (Lichtenstein 1981). Third, risk-taking is believed to be less characteristic of females than males. Studies of children (Kass 1964; Slovic 1966) and of college students (Coet and McDermott 1979) indicate lower risk-taking behaviour among females, although this finding is not always replicated (Arensen 1978). In the well-known androgyny scale constructed by Bem (1974), the willingness to take risks is defined as a masculine trait. Our culture clearly defines one aspect of masculine behaviour in terms of "daring": the derogatory term "coward" is used generally to refer to a man.

In addition, the differential occupational placement of men and women has consequences for accident mortality. Women are less likely to be employed outside the home, and when employed are more likely to be involved in relatively safe (and low-paying) "pink-collar" job settings rather than more hazardous (in terms of accidents, at any rate) blue-collar jobs. Recent evidence suggests that it is the work setting, not gender *per se*, that determines lower workplace accident rates for women (Ballau and Buchan 1978; Root and Daley 1980). Last, alcohol use is clearly related to traffic and other fatalities. It has been found that women are less likely to drink, and to drink less, than men (Ferrence 1980). Also, women are less likely to drink and drive (Carlson 1972; Storrie 1977).

In terms of cancer (malignant neoplasms), a substantial sex mortality ratio exists for cancer of the respiratory system (primarily lung cancer). The link between cigarette smoking and lung cancer is well established, and traditionally women have been less likely to smoke. While women, particularly women under the age of 25, are clearly "catching up" to men in terms of cigarette smoking (Statistics Canada 1981), current mortality statistics on respiratory cancer reflect past gender differences in smoking given that the carcinogenic effects of smoking take years to become manifest.

Gender differences in cigarette smoking are considered by some to have a substantial effect in accounting for the difference between the longevity of women and men. For example, Retherford (1975) has estimated that approximately 75 percent of the increase in the male-female differential in life expectancy (between the ages of 37 and 87) over the period from 1910 to 1962 in the United States can be accounted for by the effects of smoking. In a similar vein, Miller and Gerstein (1983) make the conclusion, based on their survey data, that differential rates of cigarette smoking are the "overwhelming" cause for the male-female longevity difference.

Gender differences in cigarette smoking also play a role in women's lower rates of mortality due to ischaemic heart disease (Waldron 1983). Another behavioural difference that has been identified as important in gender differentials in ischaemic heart disease mortality is "Type A" personality (Harrison 1978). Type A behaviour, characterized by hostility, aggression, impatience, time urgency, preoccupation with work and advancement at work, and difficulty relaxing, is clearly linked with stereotypical "ideal masculine" behaviour, and carries with it the risk of heart disease and death (Waldron 1976). It is often assumed that Type A behaviour will increase among women as they take on executive/professional work roles. However, empirical evidence suggests that women in such work roles are not at higher risk of heart disease than other women (Haynes and Feinleib 1980).

It is clear, then, that there is considerable support for the hypothesis that a large portion of women's greater longevity can be attributed to social factors associated with gender roles. Indeed, Waldron (1976) estimates that three-quarters of the difference in life expectancy can be accounted for by gender role-related behaviours. However, it is important to keep in mind that biological factors are operative as well. Gee and Veevers (1983) argue that social factors play a major role in sex mortality differentials at young ages (particularly in youth and young adulthood) but biological factors gain in importance at older ages. Also, it is likely that differences between women and men in health-related behaviours (*e.g.*, physician visits, routine check-ups), as will be discussed in the next chapter, play a role in women's greater longevity.

POLICY IMPLICATIONS

The policy implications emanating from the surplus of women relative to men among the elderly population depend upon our evaluation or judgment of the phenomenon. Is this socially problematic — something that we should try to correct?

As we will see in Chapter 4, older widowed women experience high rates of poverty. Also, widowhood itself is a traumatic experience that most women will have to face. On these grounds alone, and the additional one that men are deprived of years of life, the surplus of elderly women can be viewed as problematic for society. But we must be careful in our thinking. We must *not* assume that the problems that women face as they age will be rectified if "only" we could even up the numbers.

Could we, as a society, reduce the sex imbalance within the older age cohorts? In a facetious article written in 1980, Jacob Siegel, past-president of the Population Association of America, suggests ways that the numerical imbalance could be "corrected:" (1) encourage male births; (2) raise the death rate of women; (3) favour male immigrants; (4) lower the death rate of men. Clearly, the fourth option is the only sensible one; but how do we do it? If the social hypothesis, linking mortality levels with gender roles, is correct, even in part, then some major changes in gender role structuring will be needed. However, changes of this kind are slow to occur, given their deeply ingrained cultural and economic dimensions. However, there is nothing stopping us, in the meantime, from actively promoting better health habits and behaviours among men (and encouraging their continuation among women) such as a sensible diet, regular exercise, moderate alcohol consumption, and immediate attention to health problems.

NOTES

1. This definition of population aging is one of several definitions. See McDaniel (1986) for a discussion of the various definitions.
2. All projections relating to 2021 are derived from the 1985 Statistics Canada publication, *Population Projections for Canada, Provinces, and Territories*, Catalogue No. 91-520, using Projection 3. Projection 3 assumes: (a) fertility will stabilize by 1996 at 1.66 children per woman; (b) life expectancy at birth will increase from 71.9 in 1981 to 74.9 in 1996 and remain constant thereafter for males and increase from 79.0 to 81.6 and remain constant thereafter for females; and (c) net migration will be 100,000 per year.
3. The sex ratio, a standard demographic measurement relating the numbers of males and females in a population, is defined as the number of males per 100 females. A sex ratio of 100 means that the number of males and females is (approximately) equivalent. Values greater than 100 indicate an excess of males; values less than 100 indicate an excess of females.
4. It is important to note that the projected increase in the aged female population relative to that of the male aged male population for the period from 1981 to 2021 is highly dependent upon the assumption that future gains in female longevity will be less than gains in male longevity. The projected estimates for 2021 assume that female life expectancy will increase by 1.6 years, while male life expectancy will increase by 3 years (see note 2 of this chapter). If this assumption is incorrect, *i.e.*, if sex differences in life expectancy do not narrow, then the Canadian population in 2021 will contain considerably more females relative to males than are presented here.

CHAPTER 3

WOMEN AND HEALTH

Given the substantial sex differences in longevity, as discussed in the last chapter, we now turn our attention to the issue of sex differences in health and health-related behaviours. Also, we discuss some selected health problems that women encounter as they age, focussing upon thier psychological, sociological, and physical aspects.

The concept of health is multi-dimensional, including both physical and psychological components. It is certain that these two aspects of health interact and it is often difficult, if not impossible, to clearly separate the two dimensions. In this chapter, we will examine health in general terms although we will attempt to differentiate between psychological and physical health as much as is possible.

SEX DIFFERENCES IN HEALTH

The Empirical Evidence

It is customary (Nathanson 1975) to differentiate among three dimensions of morbidity or illness: *illness*, or reported symptoms of illness or health problems; *sick role behaviour*, or restricted activity and bed disability days; and *health service utilization*, including such aspects as medication use, physician consultations, etc.

Canadian data related to sex differences in health can be obtained from the *Canada Health Survey* and a number of government publications concerned with morbidity. It is possible to organize these data in a way that allows us to examine sex differences in terms of the above dimensions of morbidity: illness; sick role behaviour; and health service utilization. Tables 3.1 and 3.2 present data relating to *self-reported* health problems for the population aged 50 and over. It is evident that women generally report more health problems than men. While sex differences in persons reporting at least one health problem are quite small, women are substantially more likely to report a greater number of problems. However, there are certain health problems that men are more likely to report, namely, hearing disorders, heart disease, bronchitis and emphysema, and ulcers.

It will be noted that the Canada Health Survey categorization of types of health problems (Table 3.2) does not include cancer. Given that cancer is

Women and Aging

TABLE 3.1

SELF-REPORTED HEALTH PROBLEMS, MALES AND FEMALES AGED 50 AND OVER, AND SEX RATIOS, 1978-1979[1]

	Age						Sex Ratio		
	50-59		60-69		70+		(female/male) 50-59 60-69 70+		
	M	F	M	F	M	F			
Percent reporting at least one problem	68.4	77.4	79.0	85.2	85.1	89.0	1.13	1.08	1.05
Mean number of problems reported	1.4	2.0	2.1	2.5	2.3	3.0	1.43	1.19	1.30
n	1122	1188	785	879	529	726			

[1] Refers to existing conditions at the time of the interview, and therefore includes both chronic and acute conditions.

SOURCE: Special tabulations from the *Canada Health Survey* performed by the authors for this monograph.

the second leading cause of death in Canada, it is important to examine sex differences in its occurrence. Data from other governmental sources indicate that, overall, men over the age of 50 are more likely to develop cancer than their female counterparts. For example, 1980 data on the incidence of new primary sites of cancer provide sex ratios (female rate divided by male rate) of 0.95, 0.67, and 0.52 for age groups 50–59, 60–69, and 70+, respectively.[1] Data on hospital separations (hospital discharges and deaths occurring in hospital) for cancer show sex ratios of 1.14, 0.66, and 0.49 for age groups 45–64, 65–74 and 75+ respectively in 1980–81.[2] While these data are not strictly comparable with the self-reports provided in Table 3.2, it would seem that we can add cancer to the list of health problems for which older men have a preponderance. However, American data, based on interviews and hospital records, indicate that older women have higher rates of both malignant and benign neoplasms (Verbrugge 1983). There may be a national difference in this regard, but it is also possible that women in both countries have a higher incidence of less life-threatening types of malignancies.

Women are more likely than men to display sick role behaviours. (Table 3.3). They average substantially more days in bed and disability days per year. They are more likely to report some activity limitation and limitation of a major activity. However, the inability to perform a major activity is much more common among men.

A commonality emerges in the data presented so far in this chapter. In general, women report a higher frequency of health problems and disability. However, men predominate in severe disability and in some serious health conditions such as heart disease, emphysema, and, probably, the

TABLE 3.2

TYPE OF SELF-REPORTED HEALTH PROBLEMS, MALES AND FEMALES AGED 50 AND OVER, AND SEX RATIOS, 1978–1979[1]

Percent Reporting	Age 50–59 M	F	60–69 M	F	70+ M	F	Sex Ratio (female/male) 50–59	60–69	70+
Mental disorders	5.0	10.2	8.0	13.4	9.3	11.0	2.04	1.68	1.18
Endocrine disorders	3.6	9.7	7.6	13.7	6.8	13.6	2.69	1.80	2.00
Headache	3.7	10.6	4.3	8.9	1.9	4.0	2.86	2.07	2.11
Sight disorders	6.4	10.4	8.3	12.9	11.7	23.0	1.63	1.55	1.97
Hearing disorders	7.0	5.3	15.6	6.7	28.9	15.3	0.76	0.43	0.53
Hypertension	12.5	20.5	18.7	30.3	20.7	37.9	1.64	1.62	1.83
Heart disease	8.2	7.7	18.0	10.0	23.3	22.0	0.94	0.55	0.94
Acute respiratory ailments & influenza	3.7	5.9	3.7	4.8	1.7	3.9	1.59	1.30	2.29
Bronchitis & emphysema	5.0	5.0	6.9	3.9	10.0	4.7	1.00	0.57	0.47
Asthma	2.2	2.1	3.7	4.4	4.9	2.6	0.95	1.19	0.53
Hayfever & other allergies	8.0	10.0	5.0	9.1	3.4	6.9	1.25	1.82	2.03
Dental trouble	8.8	9.6	9.3	9.7	10.2	8.8	1.09	1.04	0.86
Gastric & duodenal ulcers	4.5	3.1	7.1	3.6	4.0	2.6	0.69	0.51	0.65
Digestive disorders	3.1	5.1	7.0	8.4	10.4	12.4	1.65	1.20	1.19
Skin disorders	5.3	9.3	5.1	9.0	7.8	7.2	1.75	1.76	0.92
Arthritis & rheumatism	20.4	30.6	29.8	43.8	31.5	52.6	1.50	1.47	1.67
Back, limb & joint disorders	20.4	18.7	23.8	22.5	18.9	20.2	0.92	0.95	1.07
Trauma (accidents & injury)	3.0	2.9	4.2	4.1	1.3	4.3	0.97	0.98	3.31
Other	13.4	24.0	19.7	20.1	26.5	44.1	1.79	1.47	1.66

1 Refers to existing conditions at the time of the interview and, therefore includes both acute and chronic conditions.

SOURCE: Special tabulations of the *Canada Health Survey* performed by the authors for this monograph.

virulent types of cancer. Thus, the apparent anomaly in sex differences in mortality and morbidity — "women get sick but men die" — is at least partially explained by women's greater propensity for illnesses of the non-fatal variety. The one exception is women's higher rate of diabetes; as pointed out by Gove and Hughes (1979), diabetes mellitus is the only serious condition for which women have a higher incidence than men. American data indicate that women have higher rates of illness due to acute conditions and

TABLE 3.3

SICK ROLE BEHAVIOUR, MALES AND FEMALES AGED 50 AND OVER, AND SEX RATIOS, 1978-1979[1]

	Age						Sex Ratio		
							(female/male)		
	50-59		60-69		70+		50-59	60-69	70+
	M	F	M	F	M	F			
Annual bed days per person	7.5	7.6	11.0	13.2	9.0	16.2	1.01	1.20	1.80
Annual disability days per person	20.6	28.1	33.4	35.6	27.8	40.9	1.36	1.07	1.47
Activity limitation: Percent reporting									
— no limitation	78.6	77.4	64.6	68.3	61.1	59.8	0.98	1.06	0.98
— some limitation	1.3	4.7	2.7	4.0	1.7	4.0	3.62	1.48	2.35
— major activity limited	11.1	15.2	15.7	24.1	24.8	30.0	1.37	1.53	1.21
— cannot do major activity	7.7	1.9	16.9	3.8	12.3	5.9	0.25	0.22	0.48
n	1122	1188	785	879	529	726			

SOURCE: Special tabulations of the *Canada Health Survey* performed by the authors for this monograph.

some chronic conditions but men have higher rates for a number of chronic conditions associated with high death rates (Verbrugge 1976).

Although both men and women increase their use of health services as they age, women are greater users of these services at all ages. As can be seen in Table 3.4, women are more likely to consult physicians and other health personnel and to use drugs, particularly several drugs. While men display higher rates of hospital utilization, it is possible that these data are biased by the definition of hospital separation used in Canadian sources. In Canada, hospital separation refers to both hospital discharges and deaths occurring in hospital. Thus, men's higher mortality inflates their rate of hospital separations relative to that of women. We need to have data on hospital discharges alone in order to accurately gauge sex differences in hospital utilization in Canada. We have access to such data for British Columbia (1982–83) which indicate that women aged 65 and over are lower users of hospitals with a sex ratio of .75 (Barer et al. 1986).

American data indicate higher rates of short-stay hospital utilization for older men but higher rates of institutionalization in nursing and personal care homes for older women (Kovar 1977; Verbrugge 1983). These data probably reflect, on the one hand, men's greater susceptibility to life-threatening illnesses to which they succumb and, on the other hand, the lack of a caregiver in the home for older women in conjunction with their greater longevity.

TABLE 3.4

HEALTH SERVICE UTILIZATION, MALES AND FEMALES
AGED 50 AND OVER, AND SEX RATIOS, 1978-1979[1]

	Age						Sex Ratio		
							(female/male)		
	50-59		60-69		70+		50-59	60-69	70+
	M	F	M	F	M	F			
Percent consulting physician in last year	72.9	82.2	78.1	83.0	83.6	86.9	1.13	1.06	1.04
Mean number of physician consultations in last year	3.0	4.3	5.6	6.0	5.9	6.4	1.43	1.07	1.08
Percent consulting health professional in last year	58.5	65.7	55.5	56.5	45.9	49.2	1.12	1.02	1.07
Percent using drugs[1]	48.7	66.8	57.8	73.9	71.1	80.4	1.37	1.28	1.13
Percent using three or more drug varieties[1]	6.7	15.0	11.0	22.6	14.4	26.0	2.24	2.05	1.81
Hospital separations[2] per 100,000 population, 1980-81	17,051[3]	15,768[3]	32,626[4]	24,483[4]	51,878[5]	39,643[5]	0.92	0.75	0.76

[1] Drugs refer to medicines, pills or ointments, both prescription and non-prescription.

[2] Separations refer to either discharge or death of individual cases, not persons, *i.e.*, an individual can be a case more than once in a given year.

[3] Ages 45-64.

[4] Ages 65-74.

[5] Ages 75+.

SOURCES: Special tabulations from the *Canada Health Survey* performed by the authors for this monograph; *Hospital Morbidity, 1980-81*, Statistics Canada Catalogue No. 82-206.

In general, it appears that women are "sicker" than men, *especially* in terms of milder forms of illness and disability. Women have a higher incidence of self-reported symptoms, a higher rate of sick role behaviour, and make greater use of health care services. Let us now turn to the literature that seeks to explain these phenomena.

Explanatory Models

Four major hypotheses have been put forth to account for sex differences in illness and illness-related behaviour. These hypotheses, derived from medical sociology within the United States, are all very topic-specific and do not relate, in any clear way, to the major theoretical perspectives on aging and adult development discussed in Chapter 1. The first explanation may be termed the *social acceptability* hypothesis. It argues that women are more willing to report symptoms of illness and to react to those symptoms. Our system of gender socialization and gender-related cultural expectations is deemed responsible for this differential behaviour. In terms of socialization, it is argued that females are taught that admitting, and responding to, illness symptoms is socially acceptable. According to Phillips and Segal (1969), the ethic of good health is masculine, and women, thus, are given cultural permission to be sick. This hypothesis presumes that sick role behaviour meshes with the traditional female gender role, which includes dependency as an integral component. Therefore, women feel less constrained than men to define and report mild symptoms as illness and to adopt the sick role.

A second hypothesis may be termed the *role compatibility* hypothesis. This hypothesis accounts for greater female morbidity in terms of compatibility between the sick role and women's other role responsibilities and obligations (Nathanson 1975). Basically, the idea is that it is "easier" for women to be sick. It is purported that women's roles are less demanding, thus providing them time to be "sick" and to seek cure.

A third, and somewhat related, hypothesis is the *fixed role obligations* hypothesis (Marcus and Seeman 1981b; Marcus and Siegel 1982). The postulation here is that women have fewer fixed role obligations (*i.e.*, role obligations that cannot easily be rescheduled) than men. Women have fewer work and time constraints; thus, they are freer to define themselves as ill and to reduce their activities (adopt the sick role) when feeling sick.

These three hypotheses share an underlying premise that women's higher morbidity is not "real." Women only appear to be sicker as a result of social factors that allow them a freer rein to perceive and report illness and to take on the sick role. In contrast, a fourth hypothesis asserts that women are, in fact, sicker than men and attributes the difference to strains associated with women's role in modern society. This is termed the *nurturant role hypothesis* (Gove and Hughes 1979), and holds that women, compared with men, have more role obligations that require caring for other people. The stresses associated with attending to other people's needs are purported to have a negative effect on women's health.

There is considerable lack of agreement among researchers concerning the relative merits of these four explanations. Also, it is very difficult to identify particular researchers as adherents to any given hypothesis, as there is a tendency for researchers to "switch" as new research evidence surfaces. For example, Verbrugge (1979a) argues that women are more likely to report illness symptoms (supporting the social acceptability hypothesis); by 1985, she concludes that there is no difference between women and men in reports of diagnosed chronic conditions, medical visits, and hospitalization, and that there is no convincing evidence that health reporting contributes to sex morbidity differences. In 1979, Gove is committed to the nurturant role hypothesis (Gove and Hughes 1979); by 1984, he argues that the fixed role obligations hypothesis and the nurturant role hypothesis complement one another (Gove 1984).

Such changes should not be viewed as negative; they are evidence of an exciting area of research inquiry which is evolving as new data are brought to bear on the pertinent issues. However, at present it is not possible to make any definite conclusion as to why women display higher minor morbidity than men. But we can examine some of the research findings, methodological problems, and key areas of theoretical debate bearing on the question.

Much of the data indicating higher female morbidity is obtained from surveys in which individuals provide their own reports of their health and health behaviours. Indeed, most of the data presented in this chapter is of the self-report variety. The following are some hypothesized reasons as to why this type of data may inflate levels of female illness, or deflate levels of male illness.

Verbrugge (1979a) argues that women may be more co-operative in an interview situation and try harder to recall past behaviour. Also, the use of proxy respondents can bias sex differences in illness (Mechanic 1978; Verbrugge 1979a). This technique, which was used in the Canada Health Survey, is one in which respondents provide information not only concerning themselves but also regarding other household members. It is generally agreed that proxy respondents tend to under-report the illnesses of other persons, given the difficulty of the task. Women are more likely to act as proxy respondents and, as a result, male morbidity data are underestimated (Nathanson 1977). However, a recent study (Mathiowetz and Groves 1985) suggests that the biasing effects of proxy response may be smaller than usually assumed.

The validity of the social acceptability hypothesis rests on whether or not there is convincing evidence that women are more willing to report illness symptoms, after eliminating the possible inflating effects of proxy reporting and women's purported greater willingness to co-operate in an interview situation (often called the "social desirability" effect). Phillips and Segal (1969) state that reporting illness symptoms is less stigmatizing for women and, therefore, they are more likely to do so. However, Mechanic (1978) suggests that this view is too simplistic and argues that women do not have a *generalized* tendency to report more illness symptoms, although they may be more willing to report certain types of symptoms. Gove and Hughes (1979) go even further, arguing that there is no sound empirical evidence to support the idea that women's higher rates of morbidity are a result of a differential willingness to report symptoms of ill health. However, they admit there is no strong evidence that refutes the hypothesis either. Verbrugge (1985) comes to a similar conclusion.

At present, there are no scientific grounds for either accepting or rejecting the first hypothesis. In order to come to a conclusion, researchers in the future will have to combine self-report data with clinical data.[3] While this approach is costly, it is the only way that possible sex differences in reporting behaviour can be assessed. However, it still leaves unaddressed the thorny issue of a possible sex difference in the perception of symptoms. For example, if men and women score equally on clinical measures of a disorder, but women are more likely to report symptoms of the disorder, is the difference due to reporting behaviour (*i.e.*, women are more willing to admit the problem) or to perception differences (*i.e.*, women are more likely to perceive and identify the problem as a problem)? If men are reluctant to admit and less likely to recognize a health problem, this may be an important factor in their lower life expectancy.

The second hypothesis, concerning role compatibility, is based on the premise that, in general, women have fewer role obligations and more time to take on sick role behaviour. This premise is highly suspect on two grounds. One is the empirical evidence, using time-budget methods, that indicates that women have *less* free time than men (McPherson 1985; Meissner *et al.* 1975; Szalai 1975). The other is the unstated assumption that only work in the paid labour force counts as "real" work.

The fixed role obligations hypothesis has received partial confirmation, largely from research headed by Marcus. In one study (Marcus and Seeman 1981b), it was found that fixed role obligations are related to reported disability days, but not related to self-reports of chronic conditions. In other words, women's greater flexibility in scheduling their time may be a factor in their larger number of disability days (a dimension of sick role behaviour) but is not important in relation to number of self-reported illness symptoms. In another study testing this hypothesis, Marcus *et al.* (1982) report that fixed role obligations play a larger role in determining when to relinquish the sick role as opposed to its adoption. People with fewer fixed role obligations (women, in general) will stay in bed longer when ill, but the decision to get into bed in the first place is not related to number of fixed role obligations. A third study (Marcus and Siegel 1982) found disconfirmation of the fixed role obligation hypothesis with regard to using health services for acute illnesses, and suggests that the hypothesis may be more appropriate for explaining sex differences in response to chronic symptoms.

As stated earlier, the role compatibility hypothesis and the fixed role obligation hypothesis are related. Both posit that women's role obligations lead to higher morbidity — the role compatibility hypothesis claims women have more time to be sick and the fixed role obligation hypothesis asserts that women have more flexibility in scheduling their activities around illness. These hypotheses have been useful in opening the door to an investigation of *differences among women* in morbidity. If illness is related to role obligations, it follows that women with more role obligations and more fixed role obligations will display lower morbidity. This proposition can be examined using data from the Canada Health Survey comparing employed women and homemakers on selected health indicators (Table 3.5). These data show clearly that employed women are "healthier" than homemakers. Six of the seven dimensions of health provided in Table 3.5 support this conclusion. Only on one dimension — percent consulting a physician in the last year — is there no real difference.

These Canadian data are in keeping with U.S. findings regarding the relationship between female employment and morbidity (*e.g.*, Nathanson 1975; Waldron 1980). However, even consistent findings can prove problematic in terms of their interpretation. While the data are compatible with the predictions of the role hypotheses, there are other equally tenable explanations. First, it is possible that healthier women are more likely to work outside the home in the first place (the "healthy worker" effect). The Waldron *et al.* (1982) study, using longitudinal data, found support for this effect and no evidence that labour force participation itself affects the health of middle-aged women. Second, it could be argued that women's employment leads to better health through the provision of self-esteem and social support (Nathanson 1980) as well as income.

The strongest supporters of the nurturant role hypothesis, that women are "really" physically sicker than men, are Gove and Hughes (1979). Their argument is two-fold. First, they argue that women are in poorer mental health than men and that their poorer mental health causes poorer physical health. Second, they hypothesize that women's nurturant role obligations interfere with their ability to care for themselves and lead to minor health disabilities. Although they claim empirical support for their hypothesis, their study has been strongly criticized on conceptual and methodological grounds (Mechanic 1980; Verbrugge 1980). Moreover, research sparked by the controversy (Marcus and Seeman 1981a; Wolinsky and Zusman 1981) has failed to support the conclusions of Gove and Hughes. To illustrate, Marcus and Seeman (1981a) found that women with more nurturant role obligations report *less* illness and disability, seemingly in direct contradiction to Gove and Hughes' hypothesis. However, as Marcus and Seeman point out, it is possible that the performance of nurturant roles may predispose individuals to more real illness (thus, supporting Gove and Hughes' position) but may, at the same time, inhibit the adoption of the sick role. Whether this is so remains to be seen, but the distinction made between illness and illness behaviour is an important one that must be incorporated into theory and research if an understanding of sex differences in morbidity is to be obtained.

As mentioned earlier, Gove (1984) now views the nurturant role hypothe-

TABLE 3.5

HEALTH INDICATORS FOR WOMEN AGED 50-64, BY EMPLOYMENT STATUS, 1978-1979

| | Employment Status[1] | |
| | Working in Paid | |
Illness	Labour Force	Homemaker
Percent reporting no health problems	27.9	17.4
Sick Role Behaviour		
Annual bed days per person	4.7	7.7
Anual disability days per person	17.0	31.4
Percent reporting no activity limitation	86.4	74.8
Health Services Utilization		
Percent consulting physician in last year	82.8	81.3
Mean number of physician consultations in last year	4.2	5.7
Percent using three or more drug varieties[2]	10.9	18.4
n	477	1091

[1] The retired category is omitted due to small numbers.

[2] Drugs refer to medicines, pills or ointments, both prescription and non-prescription.

SOURCE: Special tabulations from the *Canada Health Survey* performed by the authors for this monograph.

sis and the fixed role hypothesis as complementary. He sees women's higher morbidity as the joint function of the stresses of their nurturant role obligations and their lesser fixed role obligations, which make for unstructured time in which women brood over their troubles and exacerbate psychological problems which, in turn, elevate physical illness symptoms. It will be noted that Gove reinterprets the fixed role obligations hypothesis. Rather than focussing upon the freedom to be sick afforded by unstructured time, he stresses the negative mental and physical health consequences of performing roles that are amorphous and unstructured in nature.

It is clear from our preceding discussion that the jury is still out on the relative merits of the four explanations of sex differences in morbidity. It is customary in such circumstances to make a plea for further research and to move on to other topics of discussion. However, further research of the type we have been discussing may not lead to clarification of the relationship between sex and morbidity. Future research needs to take new directions, and we suggest the following.

First, *separate* theoretical explanations for sex differences in the three dimensions of morbidity — reported illness, sick role behaviour, and health service utilization — should be sought. Part of the current confusion in the literature surrounds the fact that global explanations are sought for multidimensional behaviours. Indeed, there has been a trend in recent years to examine the different aspects of morbidity separately. For example, Marcus *et al.* (1982), Marcus and Seeman (1981b) and Davis (1981) examine sex differences in reporting; Thompson and Brown (1980) and Marshall *et al.* (1982) perform research on sex differences in illness behaviour; and Hibbard and Pope (1983), Marcus and Siegel (1982), and Cleary *et al.* (1982) look at differences in health service utilization. However, except for the Marcus-led research, these studies are not directed by theoretical formulations related to the four major hypotheses concerning gender and health. Rather, new variables emerge in a one-shot fashion. To illustrate, Cleary *et al.* (1982) measure belief in preventive medicine; Thompson and Brown (1980) are concerned with identity with traditional feminine sex-role stereotypes, and Hibbard and Pope (1983) assess sex differences in interest in health. Without denying the possible validity of such variables in explaining sex differences in morbidity, there is a clear lack of theoretical integration in the limited research focussing upon the separate dimensions of morbidity.

Second, future research needs to assess the possible role of the *medical profession* in affecting sex morbidity differences. If the health problems of women and men are perceived and treated differently by medical personnel, we want to know why this is so, and what are the long-term implications for morbidity and morbidity-related behaviour. For example, we know that women are more likely to use psychotropic medication, *i.e.*, mood-altering drugs such as anti-depressants and tranquillizers (Cooperstock 1978). Given that prescription drug use is a function of the patient-physician relationship, it is crucial to know how much of the sex differences in psychotropic drug use is due to real differences in mental health and help-seeking behaviour and how much results from a tendency among physicians to prescribe such medication to women. One study (cited in Finlayson 1982) found that when men and women present identical symptoms to physicians, indicative of emotional distress, women are significantly more likely to receive tranquillizers. In a similar vein, Bernstein and Kane (1981) found that physicians are more likely to judge women's complaints as influenced by emotional factors and to identify women's health problems as psychosomatic. They suggest that the differential physician response may not be due *simply to bias against women*, but may also be a reaction to the expressive behavioural style more frequently found in women. Additionally, research by Wallen *et al.* (1979) points to doctors viewing their female patients' illnesses as psychologically caused and to physicians being more pessimistic about their recovery. This same study documents that medical information is more commonly withheld from women, thus maintaining women's dependence upon the medical profession. In contrast, Verbrugge and Steiner (1981) are doubtful that physician sex bias is common and suggest that, to the degree that it is present, it may lead to *better* health care for women. Similarly, the research of McCranie *et al.* (1978) finds no evidence of sex-role stereotyping among general practitioners.

Third, as we have seen, the theoretical concern in studies focussing on sex differentials in morbidity has been on why women are more likely than men to be sick with minor, less life-threatening illnesses. An equally important, perhaps more important, question is *why are women less likely to contract major illnesses and diseases?* This second question is related to sex differentials in mortality that favour women, as discussed in Chapter 2. It is very likely that women's greater attention to their health may be an important factor in their lower level of mortality. What is needed, then, is a theoretical approach (or approaches) that deals with sex differences in morbidity and mortality together. Such an approach would focus attention on the neglected issue of sex differences in serious illnesses and behaviours related to major illness. At the same time, the implicit focus on "sickliness as feminine" would be avoided.

Fourth, future research needs to focus on *changes in health status as individuals age* and how such changes may differ between the sexes. These research questions require longitudinal data and cannot be answered by looking at age differences in morbidity at one point in time.

HEALTH ISSUES CONCERNING OLDER WOMEN

Physical health is the single most important contributor to the quality of life for elderly women. In a study of elderly people, Himmelfarb (1984) found that physical health status was the best predictor of overall well-being. Also, a confidant protects older people against depression in the face of many losses but not in the event of severe physical illness (Lowenthal and Haven 1968). These findings apply to both women and men. Many of the issues and problems discussed in this section are relevant to both women and men; however, we have focussed where possible on issues that are either more common for older women or are exclusively female concerns.

As we discuss these specific issues, it is important to remember that a number of social and economic issues affect how older women experience health problems. Women live longer than men, they are usually poorer than men, and because their husbands die earlier, they are more likely to live alone and, in extreme old age, to be institutionalized. The older woman in poor health is less likely to have a spouse to take care of her than is the older man. She will be more dependent on other family members, particularly her daughter or daughter-in-law, to give her care. If family members are unavailable or unable to care for her, the frail elderly woman is very likely to be institutionalized. Thus, health care for the elderly woman is more likely to depend on the woman's own ability to obtain health care services — either services that are provided to her at home or services that are part of institutionalized care.

These social patterns are important to keep in mind as we interpret the research on illness in elderly women. For example, in a study of hip fractures among elderly women in nursing homes, Wyshak (1981) found that women who have four or more living children are significantly less likely to suffer hip fractures. The author concludes that the hormonal changes involved in having four or more children protects against bone loss and resulting hip fractures in old age. However, it is at least equally likely that women with four or more living children who have hip fracturers are more likely to be cared for by one of their children and, thus, not appear in a study of women in nursing homes.

Given the importance of good physical health for older women, we will first look briefly at factors that either promote or interfere with good health and then look in more detail at some specific health problems. Exercise and proper diet are two important aspects of a lifestyle that promotes good health. Although much of the data that attest to the importance of these factors is anecdotal, recent studies have shown significant improvement in the health functioning of older women as a result of increased exercise and/or a change in diet (Adams and deVries 1973; Weber *et al.* 1983). In the sections below where we discuss specific health problems, we will include specific diet and exercise information where relevant.

The use of prescription drugs, over-the-counter medications, and common substances of abuse such as alcohol and tobacco is a major deterrent to older women's health. Older people are more likely to be sensitive to drug effects, more likely to take more drugs (and therefore more likely to suffer from negative drug interactions), and take longer to eliminate any particular drug from their bodies. Some drug interactions can produce confused or psychotic states, often resulting in stronger dosages being given and even greater confusion (Hicks *et al.* 1980). Older women use more than twice as many prescription drugs and more non-prescription drugs than older men (McKim and Mishara 1987) and elderly women who live alone use more drugs than other elderly women (Porcino 1983).

A particularly important drug issue related to older women is the overprescription of tranquillizers. Women are twice as likely to receive prescriptions for tranquillizers as men. This holds true across the life-course in Canada as well as in a number of other western countries (Curran and Golombok 1985; Penfold and Walker 1983). Older women are more likely than younger women to take tranquillizers which are often prescribed for them as sleeping pills (Curran and Golombok 1985). Women are also more likely to be given repeat prescriptions. As these drugs are highly addictive, they come to feel they cannot function without them and ask their doctors for continued prescriptions.

As women are commonly defined in terms of their biology, menopause becomes viewed as a loss — both the loss of reproductive capacity and, at a biological level, the loss of estrogen. Since reproduction is seen as essential for femininity, the loss of estrogen at menopause has been viewed by the medical profession as a deficiency disease (Wilson 1966). From here it is only one step to advocating replacing estrogen in post-menopausal women.

In the 1960s a strong case was made for the routine use of estrogen replacement therapy (Wilson and Wilson 1963), and it became increasingly common in the late sixties and early seventies (Stadel and Weiss 1975; Weiss et al. 1980). Since the mid-1970s, evidence that the length of estrogen use (Mack et al. 1976; Shapiro et al. 1985; Smith, et al. 1975; Ziel and Finkle 1975) and the dosage (Mack et al. 1976) are linked to uterine cancer has produced a more balanced view of the drug. Its use has declined, but it is still a common drug therapy for menopausal and post-menopausal women and is often over-prescribed.

Like all prescription drugs, tranquillizers and estrogen, when used carefully, can benefit certain women. The problem occurs when these drugs are routinely prescribed to large numbers of elderly women.

Over-the-counter drugs are also heavily used by older women and often interact in negative ways with prescription drugs. Of particular importance are antacids and analgesics, which are commonly used by the elderly in combination with prescription drugs (Hicks et al. 1980). The use of alcohol, which is increasing among older women (Porcino 1983) not only has negative consequences in itself but also interacts negatively with many prescription and over-the-counter drugs.

Specific Health Problems of Older Women

In this section we will examine several health problems affecting older women. In the space available here, it is not possible to cover all of the many health problems that older women encounter. In choosing the illnesses to include here — depression, Alzheimer's Disease, osteoporosis, and breast cancer — we have used the following criteria: (1) all of these illnesses affect women more than men; (2) they affect large numbers of women; and (3) when they occur they create major physical and mental disturbances in the individual woman's life and in some cases are life-threatening.

Depression

Approximately twice as many women as men are depressed. This finding is reported both within psychiatric populations and in community surveys (Curran and Golombok 1985; Penfold 1981; Stoppard et al. 1986). In the past it was assumed that depression was a common problem of older women, particularly those experiencing menopause. There was even a specific diagnosis for it — Involutional Melancholia (Penfold 1981). However, studies indicate that menopausal women are not at greater risk of depression (McKinlay and Jefferys 1974; Rosenthal 1968; Winokur 1973) and the diagnosis of Involutional Melancholia has been removed from more recent psychiatric diagnostic manuals. In constrast to earlier views, it is housewives with preschool children who are at highest risk (Penfold 1981).

Working-class housewives in this situation are more likely to be depressed than middle-class housewives (Curran and Golombok 1985). Isolation, high performance demands, and lack of social status associated with being alone in the home with small children are cited as factors that contribute to depression.

Data concerning sex differences in depression among older women and men are not readily available. Statistics Canada (1984a) reports diagnostic data by sex and age for mental and psychiatric hospital separations. These data (1981–82) show that in the categories of affective psychosis and depressive disorders, not elsewhere classified, women aged 45 and over outnumber men by approximately 50 percent. These data are consistent with the proposition that more older women than older men are depressed. However, most people who are treated for depression go to general rather than psychiatric hospitals. Thus, these data present a very partial picture.

In a study of older, community-dwelling women and men, Himmelfarb (1984) found that women endorsed more depressive symptoms than men. When he controlled for a number of variables including physical health, social support, and stressful life-events, women and men did not differ in depressive symptoms. This implies that sex differences in depression among this group of elderly are related to other life differences which presumably leave women at a disadvantage relative to men. These results are consistent with the feminist view that women show more depression because they have more depressing lives.

Even though older women are not the highest risk group among women in terms of depression, it can be a severe and often unnoticed problem for some older women, particularly those who live alone. Depression is the most common functional mental disorder of later adulthood and it is estimated that as many as 30 percent of older adults experience at least one period of mild depression (Perlmutter and Hall 1985). The depressed person feels inadequate, hopeless, blames herself harshly, has problems sleeping, lacks energy, loses interest in everyday activities, has trouble thinking and making decisions, and sometimes has suicidal thoughts (Penfold and Walker 1983). In older people, depressive symptomology tends to be flat and monotonic with an emphasis on fatigue and bodily complaints (Stenback 1980). Because pessimism, passivity, and bodily complaints are often stereotyped as normal in the elderly, many elderly people may be depressed and yet go unnoticed by doctors and other professionals. This may be particularly true of women who live alone.

Depression is not only psychologically disturbing, it also often involves a loss of appetite and the desire to care for oneself that can lead to physical declines which in turn lead to further depression. Also, older women are likely to be taking several prescription drugs in addition to over-the-counter drugs which may, in their interaction, induce depression.

Alzheimer's Disease

Alzheimer's affects approximately twice as many elderly women as men (Spar 1982). This difference is probably related to women's greater longevity, as Alzheimer's is more common at advanced ages. Alzheimer's affects 5 to 10 percent of people over the age of 65 and 10 to 20 percent of people over 75 (Powell 1985). Alzheimer's is a form of chronic brain dysfunction and as such is irreversible. It is impossible to diagnose Alzheimer's with certainty until an autopsy is conducted after death. An accurate diagnosis involves the elimination of other possibilities such as metabolic disorders, drug-induced dementia, depression, or toxicity.

The Alzheimer's victim moves through four phases. In the first phase, it is not clear that anything is wrong. The person seeks familiar situations, may be slow in reacting or learning new things, and is easily upset and angered when words are lost. In the second phase, more losses occur. Speech is slowed, misunderstanding occurs in everyday conversation, and the victim may need help with everyday activities such as balancing a chequebook. Making decisions becomes increasingly difficult and forgetfulness increases. In the third phase, disability is marked. The victim loses normal orientation of time and place and fails to identify familiar people. In the fourth phase, the person loses both recent and distant memories, is often unable to recognize herself or other familiar people, and needs help with daily care activities (Powell 1985).

The disease is a painful and frustrating one for both the victim and the caregiver. Both need help in dealing with anger and frustration. Since women live longer than men and are more likely to live alone, women with Alzheimer's are less likely to be living with someone who can care for them during the earlier stages of Alzheimer's and thus more likely to be institutionalized.

Osteoporosis

Osteoporosis is a disease resulting from excessive bone loss. It is primarily a female disease; it has been estimated that one in four women over the age of 60 suffers from osteoporosis (Notelovitz and Ware 1982). In osteoporosis, the loss of bone mass leads to weakened bones which break more easily. The most common fractures are of the spinal vertebrae, wrist, and hip. The first fractures usually occur in the spine as one or more vertebrae collapse on each other. These fractures are usually not the result of a major stress to the spine, but often occur during normal bending or lifting movements. The fracture occurs because the bone mass in the spine decreases below the critical level needed to support the weight of the body (Whedon 1981).

The fractures result in a shortening of the spine, an inward curvature of the lower spine, and an outward curvature of the upper spine. In severe cases of osteoporosis, height loss of 10 cm or more can occur (Kaplan 1985; Notelovitz and Ware 1982). The woman's posture changes significantly, resulting in the "dowager's hump" and a protruding abdomen. This curvature of the spine decreases the size of the abdominal cavity, crowds the internal organs, and results in a decreased tolerance of exercise and difficulty with digestion (Kaplan 1985).

Osteoporosis is both physically and psychologically debilitating. The pain associated with vertebral fractures can be severe and long lasting. Movement and exercise, which are important to reduce further bone loss, become difficult and anxiety-inducing due to a fear of further fractures. Postural changes lead to significant distortion in body shape that can be distressing. Clothes no longer fit and it is very difficult to buy clothes that do. A woman's body image often becomes quite negative.

Osteoporosis can also be life threatening. The most directly life-threatening risk is that of hip fracture or, more accurately, a fracture of the upper part of the thigh bone (femur). Not only is a hip fracture severely debilitating in itself, it can, through resulting complications, lead to death. It is estimated that 15 percent of women who suffer a hip fracture die shortly after the injury and almost 30 percent die within a year (Notelovitz and Ware 1982). One estimate is that a hip fracture reduces a woman's life expectancy by 12 percent (Notelovitz and Ware 1982).

Osteoporosis is a woman's disease. Women enter early adulthood with a lower bone mass than men and, therefore, begin the process of bone loss at a lower starting point. In addition, women lose bone at a faster rate than men. After the age of 40, men lose about .50 to .75 percent of their bone mass per year while for women the figures range from 1.5 to 2.0 percent (Kaplan 1985). After the age of 65, this rate of decline slows down for women to about 3 to 4 percent per decade (Boston Women's Health Book Collective 1984; Notelovitz and Ware 1982). It is estimated that by the time a woman is 80 years old, she will have lost 47 percent of her trabecular[4] bone while a man will have lost only 14 percent (Notelovitz and Ware 1982). Why women lose bone mass at a higher rate is not clear. Much has been made of the relationship between loss of bone mass and loss of estrogen during menopause. However, the data that correlate bone loss with estrogen loss are unclear. Since women lose bone at a faster rate than men before menopause, factors other than estrogen contribute to women's greater bone loss.

It is difficult to estimate rates of bone loss from these studies since they are all cross-sectional; cohort as well as age changes may account for the results. Since more recent cohorts are taller and, therefore, have greater bone mass, age differences observed represent cohort differences as well as age changes.

Osteoporosis has been shown to relate to a number of factors relevant to the attainment and maintenance of bone mass. Heredity is one factor that is important in determining osteoporosis. Women who develop osteoporosis are more likely to have a family history of it than women who do not (Notelovitz and Ware 1982). Also, black women have a greater bone mass than white women at maturity and, therefore, are protected against subsequent bone loss which appears to occur at a constant rate for both races (Kaplan 1985).

Other factors which are important relate to lifestyle, in particular diet and exercise. Exercise, particularly weight-bearing exercise such as walking, aerobics, running, bicycling, and weight lifting[5] both lead to greater peak bone mass in young women and retard bone loss in older women. An interesting related factor is that osteoporosis occurs less in heavy women. This may be partly related to estrogen production (Notelovitz and Ware 1982), but is also due to the greater weight-bearing exercise heavy women get in everyday activities.

Another factor that is critical to attaining and maintaining bone mass is diet. Probably the most critical dietary element is calcium. A woman's need for calcium intake increases with age because her body becomes less able to absorb and use the calcium she consumes. Adequate vitamin D intake is necessary for calcium absorption. Vitamin D in natural sources comes from exposure to sunshine, fish liver oils, and in milk which is fortified with vitamin D (Kaplan 1985).

Smoking has been positively linked to osteoporosis. Post-menopausal women who smoke have significantly more vertebral compression fractures than non-smokers. Furthermore, women aged 60–69 show more bone loss if they smoke and this increases for smokers who are also less than 10 percent overweight (Daniell 1976).

Several forms of treatment for osteoporosis are possible. The simplest treatment with the fewest side effects is calcium supplements and increased exercise. Calcium supplements have been shown to reduce bone loss in post-menopausal women (Recker *et al.* 1977) and to reduce the number of vertebral fractures in women with osteoporosis (Riggs *et al.* 1982).

Another possibility is estrogen replacement therapy as estrogen, or estrogen plus progesterone, has been clearly related to decreased bone loss (Aitken *et al.* 1973; Christiansen *et al.* 1980; Lindsay *et al.* 1976; Recker *et al.* 1977) and decreased risk of fractures (Riggs *et al.* 1982; Weiss *et al.* 1980).

The problem with the use of estrogen is, as already discussed, the increased risk of uterine cancer. Furthermore, if estrogen is to protect against bone loss, it should be taken for a long period of time, since termination of estrogen therapy is correlated with rapid bone loss (Boston Women's Health Book Collective 1984; Lindsay *et al.* 1978). However, length of estrogen use is correlated with increased risk of uterine cancer.

Breast Cancer

Breast cancer is a life-threatening disease that strikes one out of 11 women at some time in their lives. Although breast cancer is more common in post-menopausal women, they have a better chance of survival than younger women (Boston Women's Health Book Collective 1984). For women of all ages, the main fear associated with breast cancer is the fear of death. For women who have undergone a surgical procedure in which all of the breast is removed, there is also psychological threat to body image and self-esteem. It is often assumed that the loss of one or both breasts is less traumatic for older women. However, both older and younger women who have lost a breast need to make a major psychological adjustment. The role played by sexual partners is important to this adjustment (Lorde 1980; Spletter 1982).

Whenever a woman discovers a lump in her breast her first fear is cancer. However, in the vast majority of cases the lump turns out to be benign. The general medical term for lumps in the breast is fibrocystic disease. Love *et al.* (1982) have questioned whether a tendency to lumpy breasts (which occurs clinically in 50 percent of women and histologically in 90 percent) should be called a disease. They suggest that perhaps "lumpy breasts" or "physiologic nodularity" are more accurate terms that would encourage the study of breast physiology and anatomy without the negative connotation of disease.

One of the reasons that the term disease has been used is the assumption that the presence of benign lumps puts a woman at a greater risk of developing cancer of the breast. However, the increased risk for women with benign breast conditions compared to women without benign breast conditions is very small (Dupont and Page 1985; Love *et al.* 1982). Only one woman in 50 who has breast cancer has had a previous biopsy of breast tissue (Hutter 1985).

All women are "at risk" of getting breast cancer and very few factors increase this risk significantly. No risk factor predicts for an individual woman whether she will get cancer. In 75 percent of breast cancers, none of the "risk factors" are present. Furthermore, many women who belong to a high risk group never get cancer (Boston Women's Health Book Collective 1984). Of the many demographic and health history factors studied, the only ones that have been shown to significantly increase risk are: (1) if a mother or sister had breast cancer in one breast before the age of 40 (the risk increases if the cancer was in both breasts); (2) exposure to large doses of radiation or exogenous estrogens; and (3) a previous personal history of breast cancer (Boston Women's Health Book Collective 1984).

The understanding of breast cancer as a disease has changed considerably over the past few years. In the past, it was commonly believed that breast cancer began as a localized disease in the breast and spread from there to other parts of the body. The treatment that paralleled this view emphasized early detection and removal of a large amount of breast and surrounding tissue. However, more recently, researchers are beginning to realize that at least some forms of breast cancer are systemic — the cancer is present in other parts of the body before it appears as a lump in the breast.

With the change in view of the nature of breast cancer, the advantages of early detection are called into question. While early detection is probably useful for more localized kinds of cancer, the advantages for systemic cancer are less obvious. If the cancer already exists elsewhere in the body before it is found in the breast, the main result of early detection may be increased time that one is aware of having cancer but not increased survival (Boston Women's Health Book Collective 1984).

One of the main tools used in early detection of breast cancer is the mammogram or x-ray of the breast. A problem with the mammogram is that it is not 100 percent accurate. The false positive rate (indicating cancer when none is present) is about 7 percent and the false negative rate (missing a cancer which is present) ranges from 4–30 percent. Some women with false positives have had mastectomies (Boston Women's Health Book Collective 1984). Although the advantage of the mammogram is that it may detect cancers too small to be felt, this type of cancer is most likely to be a minimal or slow-growing one — the kind that would not be life-threatening without treatment. Thus, detection of cancers through the mammogram may result in some unnecessary treatments which will inflate the cure and survival rates in early detection studies (Boston Women's Health Book Collective 1984).

Until quite recently the treatment most used for breast cancer was the Halstead or radical mastectomy in which all the breast tissue, lymph nodes, and chest muscle was removed. The use of the Halstead was more common in the United States than in Canada or European countries (Boston Women's Health Book Collective 1984). This treatment was based on the assumption that the tumour was localized, and that the more of the surrounding tissue that was removed, the better the chance that the cancer would not spread. Given what is now known about the systemic nature of some breast cancers, it is not surprising that cure rates for breast cancer did not improve with the use of the radical mastectomy and comparisons with untreated groups did not show a clear advantage to the treatment (Henderson and Canellos 1980; Mueller 1985). In addition, significant negative physical and psychological effects accompany radical mastectomy, including the emotional trauma of losing a breast, scarring, posture and balance problems, arm problems such as fatigue, swelling, and inability to raise the arm or carry heavy items, and a reduced resistance to infection (Boston Women's Health Book Collective 1984).

Treatment alternatives for breast cancer are particularly important to women psychologically because of the consequences for body image and self-esteem resulting from having part or all of a breast (or breasts) removed. In addition to the ever-present fear of a recurrence of cancer, after surgery a woman must make decisions about wearing a prosthesis and having breast reconstruction. In making these decisions, women often report very negative feedback from doctors, nurses, and others for their decisions. In a double bind, women who have had a breast removed may be criticized either for not wearing a prosthesis and, thus, refusing to look "normal" (Lorde 1980), or for wanting breast reconstruction, instead of a prosthesis, in order to look and feel "normal" (Spletter 1982).

Menopause

Myths surrounding menopause have created a stereotype of it as a psychologically difficult or crisis time for women. Women are assumed to be depressed (Penfold 1981) because of hormonal changes, loss of reproductive capacity, or because their youngest child leaves home, thus marking an end to their role as mother (Bart 1971). Numerous studies indicate that none of these factors are related to psychological crises in middle-aged women. As seen in our discussion of depression, this is not a time when women are especially vulnerable to depression. Hormone changes are in themselves not linked to depression (Penfold and Walker 1983). Only a small minority of women regrets the loss of childbearing capacity (Neugarten *et al.* 1963) and most experience the empty nest (see Chapter 6 for a more detailed discussion of the empty nest) with relief (Rubin 1979). Most women experience menopause as having a positive outcome, and the most negative statement among menopausal women is a fear of the unknown (Neugarten *et al.* 1963). Consistent with the view that the stereotypes around menopause are more negative than the experience itself is the finding that younger women are significantly more negative in their attitudes than are menopausal women (Neugarten *et al.* 1963).

To the extent that menopause is significant in a woman's life, it is so as a biological rather than a social or psychological event. The major biological change that occurs with menopause is a decrease in the production of estrogen by the ovaries.[6] Three physical consequences are clearly linked to the decrease in estrogen. One is changes in the menstrual cycle. Some women menstruate more frequently; others experience a decrease in their periods. Increased menstrual irregularity, accompanied by break-through bleeding, is not uncommon. Some women even experience pre-menstrual tension for the first time. For one-fifth of women, there are no changes until menstruation suddenly and completely stops (Boston Women's Health Book Collective 1984).

The second consequence is the hot flash. Hot flashes are caused by the irregular and unpredictable dilation and constriction of blood vessels. While hot flashes have been clearly linked to the decrease in estrogen, not all menopausal women experience them, and among those that do, the severity of the discomfort is highly varied. For the minority of women who experiences severe hot flashes, they can be very debilitating, causing disrupted sleep, embarrassment, severe sweating and chills, or feelings of suffocation (Boston Women's Health Book Collective 1984).

The third physical consequence linked to decreased estrogen is atrophy of the vaginal wall or epithelium. When this occurs women experience an itchiness or dryness in the vagina, and intercourse can be painful. Again not all women experience vaginal atrophy; it is a serious symptom for only a minority of women.

It is not clear now how many women experience these menopausal symptoms. The percentages reported vary from a low of 10 to 15 percent to a high of 50 percent (Posner 1979). With such a range it is difficult to know just how frequent and severe these symptoms are for women. The range is probably partly accounted for by differing definitions: a study counting all women who report any symptoms to their doctors will give a very different figure than a study that includes only those women who are incapacitated by their symptoms. Even if one chooses the highest figure, one-half of women are symptom-free in menopause.

POLICY IMPLICATIONS

As our population ages, we can expect higher proportions of people with health problems. Given that our population will comprise a higher proportion of women, particularly at the older ages, when health care needs increase, and that women, for reasons that are still not clear, are greater users of health care services, we seem to face a future in which the costs of health care will escalate. However, before we accept such a scenario for the future as proposed, let us consider two issues. First, there is currently a trend away from curative medicine towards preventive medicine. While preventive medicine requires education of the public and a commitment by individuals to control and take responsibility for their own health, these trends are already surfacing. To the degree that preventive self-directed care increases, the overall health care costs of an aging population may not be as great as what would be extrapolated from past trends. Second, some of the evidence presented in this chapter suggests that women who are "integrated" into mainstream society have fewer health problems than women in the traditional female role. As gender roles change, and as more women are provided with opportunities to exercise control over their lives and power in society generally, the female preponderance in morbidity may decline.

It seems likely that both factors — increased preventive measures and increased female involvement in society — will create "healthier" women at all stages of the life-course. Even so, with advancing age health problems increase, and societal resources will have to be allocated to ensure that tomorrow's older women receive adequate health care. Particularly relevant is the fact that frail elderly women over the age of 75 are twice as likely to be institutionalized in long-term care facilities, the combined results of their health care needs and the absence of a care-giving spouse. Our current health care system, based on an acute care model, must be revised (Chappell *et al.* 1986). Hess (1985) suggests that such a revision would have occurred long ago if men were the ones who found themselves in nursing homes in old age.

NOTES

1. These ratios are calculated from data provided in *Cancer in Canada, 1980*, Statistics Canada Catalogue No. 82-207.
2. These ratios are calculated from data provided in *Hospital Morbidity, 1980–81*, Statistics Canada Catalogue No. 82-206.
3. The one study we were able to find that combines self-report and clinical data reports no differences between women and men in the reporting of osteoarthritic symptoms (Davis 1981). On the other hand, data from the Canadian Health Survey on hypertension are suggestive of a reporting difference. Among the sample aged 65 and over, 11.4 percent of men and 26.0 percent of women report having hypertension. However, the actual testing of blood pressure revealed that 13.7 percent of men and 9.1 percent of women had elevated diastolic readings (readings greater than 95 millimetres) and 15.9 percent of men and 14.7 percent of women had elevated systolic readings (readings greater than 165 millimetres). The pertinent fact here is that while women are more likely to report high blood pressure, actual tests reveal that a larger proportion of men has it.
4. The two main kinds of bone structures are called *cortical* and *trabecular*. Cortical bone is solid and dense in structure compared to trabecular bone which is more porous with a latticework structure. All bones contain both types of structures, but in varying proportions. The spine, for example, consists mostly of trabecular bone while the long bones of the arm and leg consist mostly of cortical bone with trabecular bone concentrated at the ends of the bones. Both kinds of bones are susceptible to age-related bone loss, but trabecular bone, with its greater surface area, is more vulnerable. Thus, most of the injuries that result from bone loss take place in trabecular bone (the spine and the ends of the long bones of the arm and leg).
5. Swimming, which is an excellent aerobic exercise, is not as helpful in generating and preserving bone mass because the water supports one's weight. It is certainly better than no exercise, but not as good in this respect as walking or other weight-bearing exercise. For women who already suffer from osteoporosis, swimming is sometimes the exercise of choice since it is less likely to stress the bones and cause further injury.

6. Women who have a hysterectomy in which the uterus is removed, but the ovaries are not, will not experience this decrease in estrogen even though they no longer menstruate. This would suggest that a more accurate definition of menopause, in terms of biological consequences, is decrease in estrogen production by the ovaries rather than the cessation of menstruation.

CHAPTER 4

OLDER WOMEN AND INCOME: THE PROBLEM OF POVERTY

In recent years, a view that the economic situation of elderly people has improved substantially and, indeed, that most older people are relatively well-off, has surfaced. Such prominent social scientists as Kingsley Davis (Davis and van den Oever 1981) and Samuel Preston (1984) have made this claim, mirroring sentiments expressed in the popular media. Both argue that the economic gains made by the elderly have occurred at the expense of other age groups — children, in the case of Preston, and younger workers, in the case of Davis. However, as pointed out by Binstock (1983), the view of the elderly as a reasonably well-off segment of society has a number of flaws. Most notably, this view does not take into account the economic diversity of the older population; it diverts attention away from issues of economic reform; and it functions, at a time of economic recession and uncertainty, as a scapegoating mechanism — the aged, or at least their growing numbers, become viewed as a major reason for economic stagnation.

As we shall see shortly, it is true that older people, *as a whole*, are better off now than in the past. It is the case that a small *portion* of elderly people is very or quite well-off financially. For example, in 1982 approximately 11 percent of men and 3.5 percent of women aged 65 and over had incomes of $25,000 or more (National Council of Welfare 1984b). However, it is also true that older women, particularly older women who are not or are no longer married, have not shared equally in these gains and cannot, for the most part, be characterized as financially secure. In other words, if we do not view the elderly as a homogeneous entity and if we examine the economic conditions of sub-groups within the aged population, we find a diverse picture in terms of financial condition.

THE INCIDENCE OF POVERTY

Measuring Poverty

The measurement of poverty is fraught with difficulties, and has been approached in a number of ways. The most common method is to use an absolute standard, such as the "poverty line." This has been the approach used in Canada.

Three separate bodies in Canada — Statistics Canada, the Canadian Council on Social Development, and the Senate Committee on Poverty — have established poverty lines. All vary their poverty lines according to family size, but base their estimates on differing definitions of poverty.

Statistics Canada poverty lines are based on a subsistence conception of poverty. Any individual or family that spends 58.5 percent or more of total income on the necessities of life — food, shelter and clothing — is considered poor.[1] Statistics Canada also varies its low income cut-offs according to size of place of residence, with lower cut-offs for rural areas and higher cut-offs as size of place of residence increases. The Canadian Council on Social Development bases its poverty lines on income inequality. Individuals and families are considered poor if they live on less than half of the average income. The Senate Committee on Poverty uses an approach that combines elements of the other two measures. Like Statistics Canada, the Senate Committee bases its poverty lines on expenditure, rather than income. However, unlike Statistics Canada, the Senate Committee poverty lines are based on a conception of income adequacy rather than subsistence.

The three approaches produce quite different poverty lines. In 1981, for a family of two, the Statistics Canada poverty line was $8,595,[2] the Canadian Council on Social Development poverty line was $10,357, and the Senate Committee on poverty line was $11,600 (National Council of Welfare 1981). We will be using Statistics Canada poverty lines in this chapter, largely because a greater range of types of data are available from this source. However, it must be kept in mind that these poverty lines are the least "generous," and quite probably *under-estimate* the incidence of poverty.

Poverty Among Older Women

In 1981, of Canada's 1,350,000 women aged 65 and over, 415,000, or approximately 31 percent, lived at or below the poverty line. This figure compares with 19 percent for men aged 65 and over. While the disparity between women and men is obvious, both figures are *conservative* in that they are based on Statistics Canada poverty lines which, as noted above, are the least generous. Also, they do not include the Yukon, Northwest Territories, Indian reserves, and institutions such as old age homes (National Council of Welfare 1984b). It is a virtual certainty that *more than one-third* of Canada's elderly women are poor.

The likelihood of poverty in old age is closely related to family status. Women who live in families, especially in families with a man present (or, in census terminology, a male head) do not have a high poverty rate. (Table 4.1). Indeed, in 1982, only 11.7 percent of families with an aged head lived

TABLE 4.1

INCIDENCE OF POVERTY FOR FAMILIES AND UNATTACHED INDIVIDUALS, BY SEX, POPULATION AGED 65+, 1982

	Poor[a]		Not Poor	
	Number	%	Number	%
Families				
Female head	21,000	24.6	64,366	75.4
Male head	77,000	10.2	677,902	89.8
Total	98,000	11.7	742,268	88.3
Unattached Individuals[b]				
Female	337,000	60.4	220,947	39.6
Male	85,000	48.9	88,824	51.1
Total	422,000	57.7	309,369	42.3

[a] Statistics Canada definition of poverty (1978 base).

[b] Individuals who live alone or in households with unrelated persons.

SOURCE: National Council of Welfare 1984b.

in poverty, which is less than the figure for families with a head aged under 65 years, 14.2 percent. Nevertheless, it will be noted that aged families with a female head are much more likely to be poor (24.6 percent) than families with a male head (10.2 percent).

It is unattached elderly persons who are most likely to be poor. Over 60 percent of unattached women aged 65 and over existed at or below the poverty line in 1982. The figure for unattached elderly men is high as well (48.9 percent), but there are nearly four times more unattached elderly women than men. These unattached elderly women are, for the most part, widows, and their likelihood of being poor increases with advancing age, In 1981, 65 percent of unattached women aged 70 and over were poor (National Council of Welfare 1984b).

So far, we have been examining percentages of persons (and families) existing at or below the poverty line. There is also a substantial portion of elderly who may be classified as "near poor," who have incomes just over the arbitrary poverty line. In 1983, the Statistics Canada poverty line was approximately $8,000 for an individual (National Council of Welfare 1984a). Approximately 60 percent of elderly unattached women have incomes at or below that figure but an additional 18 percent have incomes between $8,000 and $9,999 (Statistics Canada 1985). Thus, approximately 78 percent of older unattached women are poor or "near poor." The comparable figure for unattached elderly men is approximately 68 percent. It is clear that being "unattached" is economically disadvantageous for both older women and men — elderly men do not fare much better than their female counterparts — but a crucial issue is that there are so many more older women in this category.

The estimation of "near-poverty" among the elderly living in families is problematic because of variations in family size. However, let us assume that the average family size for a family with a head aged 65 and over is 2.5. The 1983 poverty line for such a family was approximately $12,000. Approximately 22 percent of families with an aged head had an income between $12,000 and $14,999 in 1983 (Statistics Canada 1985). Adding this percent to the percent of aged poor families (11.7 percent) implies that about one-third of families with a head aged 65 years and over are poor or "near poor."

Examining trends in poverty, we can see that progress has been made (Table 4.2). However, that progress is very uneven. Poverty among aged families has declined quite dramatically, *except* for families with an aged female head. Indeed, for this category, the incidence of poverty has increased in recent years. For unattached individuals, a trend of declining rates of poverty is evident, but to a greater degree for men than for women.

TABLE 4.2

TRENDS IN POVERTY FOR FAMILIES AND UNATTACHED INDIVIDUALS, POPULATION AGED 65+, 1969-1982

| | Percent in Poverty[a] | | | | |
| | Families | | | Unattached Individuals[b] | |
	Female Head	Male Head	Total	Women	Men
1969[c]	*	*	41.4	69.1[d]	
1979	22.2	21.8	21.9	68.8	58.6
1980	21.2	13.3	14.2	65.4	51.9
1981	24.7	12.9	14.5	62.2	48.4
1982	24.6	10.2	11.7	60.4	48.9
Percent change 1979-82	+10.8	−53.2	−46.6	−12.2	−16.5

* data not available

[a] Statistics Canada definition of poverty.

[b] Individuals who live alone or in households with unrelated members.

[c] The figures for 1969 are based on a different definition of the poverty line and should be viewed as only roughly comparable to the later figures.

[d] Combined percent for women and men.

SOURCE: National Council of Welfare 1984b.

To summarize, we have seen that the income level of elderly Canadians is quite diverse, but that large numbers of women are poor or near poor. This is especially true of the 557,947 older women who are unattached — approximately 78 percent of them live in or near poverty. Also, these women are not making comparable progress in their income level, relative to other groups. Elderly women who head families (approximately 21,000 women) are actually experiencing a worsening income situation, with a trend toward an increase in the percentage in poverty.

To understand why the incomes of the elderly, particularly elderly women, are so low, it is useful to examine the sources of their income.

The government is an important source of income for elderly Canadians. For elderly couples and for unattached men, public sources comprise approximately 46 percent of their income (Table 4.3). Among elderly unattached women, there is a greater reliance on public monies.

TABLE 4.3

SOURCES OF INCOME FOR COUPLES AND UNATTACHED INDIVIDUALS, POPULATION AGED 65+, 1981

		Unattached Individuals[b]	
Source	Couples[a]	Women	Men
Old Age Security/Guaranteed Income Supplement	33.5	42.7	32.3
Other government sources	2.8	3.2	3.5
Canada/Quebec Pension Plan	9.2	7.4	10.8
Total Public Sources	45.5	53.3	46.6
Private Pensions	11.6	8.8	16.0
Investments	27.9	31.2	27.6
Employment	13.9	4.8	8.5
Total Private Sources	54.5	46.7	53.4
Total	100.0	100.0	100.0

a Couples in which both spouses are aged 65 or over.

b Individuals who live alone or in households with unrelated members.

SOURCE: National Council of Welfare 1984b.

Among the poor elderly, either in families or unattached individuals, approximately 90 percent of income is derived from government sources — Old Age Security, the Guaranteed Income Supplement and provincial supplements[3] (National Council of Welfare 1984b). In 1983, due to varying amounts of provincial supplements, maximum government money ranged, for a single person, from $6,147 to $7,347 and, for a couple, from $10,883 to $13,283 (National Council of Welfare 1984b). These amounts do not equal the 1983 poverty line of $8,305 for a single person and only slightly exceed the poverty line of $10,920 for a couple (National Council of Welfare 1984a). The fact that one-half of Canada's elderly — over 700,000 women and 500,000 men — have so little income that they qualify for the Guaranteed Income Supplement indicates the magnitude of the problem.

It is sometimes argued that a focus on money income alone portrays an overly pessimistic picture of the financial situation of elderly persons. Such a focus does not take into account such variables as: non-money sources of income; the fact that most older people do not have to incur employment-related expenses; special federal tax concessions; the indirect financial benefits of our national health insurance system; elderly discounts for transportation, entertainment and certain consumer items; and equity from home ownership. While it is important not to forget these non-cash sources of income, it is also important to keep in mind that our elderly population does not share in them equally. For example, an elderly woman, probably a widow, living at or below the poverty line will not benefit from special tax exemptions (she will not have enough income to file a tax return!), nor will she benefit from a $2.00 reduction on a theatre ticket if she cannot afford to get to the theatre or pay the discounted price once there. It has been estimated that non-money sources of income, including receipts-in-kind and provision of services by children and other relatives, can add up to 30 percent more to the income of aged persons (Stone and Fletcher 1980). However, it has been pointed out (Health and Welfare Canada 1982c) that most of this 30 percent is in the form of transfers to married women by their husbands. Thus, older unattached women receive less non-money income than their better-off peers.

In terms of home ownership, a mixed picture emerges. Among elderly women, approximately one-half are homeowners and one-half are renters; however, with increasing age, Canadian women are more likely than men to be renters (Connidis and Rempel 1983). Among elderly female homeowners, many are "house rich but cash poor." Their home is their most valuable asset, but its maintenance takes a large portion of their income. Selling their homes would be only a temporary solution to their financial problems, leaving them no better off in the long run (National Council of Welfare 1984b). Of course, some elderly women own expensive homes. For them, selling their home would be more financially beneficial, but they are less likely to need to sell their homes to obtain cash.

FACTORS ACCOUNTING FOR WOMEN'S POVERTY IN LATER LIFE

There has been surprisingly little theoretical work by social scientists on the issue of women's poverty in later life. There is a considerable amount of data collected by government sources and there are a number of descriptive reports such as the National Council of Welfare's (1984b) *Sixty-Five and Over*. Also, there are a number of reports calling for reform in our pension system generally, and for women, culminating in the federal Green Paper on pensions, *Better Pensions for Canadians* (Health and Welfare Canada 1982a). But there is very little research that examines this problem theoretically. In this section we attempt to examine the poverty of older women using a combined feminist/interpretive perspective. Throughout, it will be shown that many of the variables that have led to high rates of poverty among the present population of older women continue to operate for younger women. In other words, future cohorts of elderly women are likely to experience high levels of poverty as well, although perhaps not as high as today's older women.

Women's Life-long Dependent Status

It is clear that our society is organized on the premise that women will be financially "cared for" by men. As pointed out by Tindale *et al.* (1983), many women live on the margins of poverty throughout their lives. However, most women marry and their *personal poverty* is masked behind measures of household income. This personal poverty becomes evident when marriages break up due either to divorce or widowhood. Most women, regardless of their age, who are "man-less" are poor or close to it. In fact, the poverty rate of non-aged female-headed families approaches 50 percent (National Council of Welfare 1984b). Thus, elderly women are not poor because they are old; they are poor because they are women who outlive their husbands. Of course, not all older widows are poor; those who are not poor are not poor because their husbands were financially well-off and left them well "provided for." Either way — whether the latter years of life are comfortable or a fight for basic needs — the economic situation of older women, particularly widows, is closely tied to, even dependent upon, their husbands' financial status and/or longevity.

Womens' dependent status throughout their lives is a direct result of our gender-based division of labour. Men work outside the home, and control the power resources of the wider society.[4] Women work inside the home, and wield little power in the broader society. As domestic work is unpaid, it carries minimal value in a society which equates worth with money, protestations about the importance of "bringing up the next generation" notwithstanding. Even when women work outside the home, this work is viewed as secondary to the primacy of their domestic duties. Thus, women have a devalued role in our society: both their domestic labour and their outside-the-home labour is discounted. Lacking social and economic power, women have little choice but to rely upon (be dependent upon) men.

This dependence is reinforced by a dominant ideology that views men as superior and that stresses individualism ("you can make it if you try"). If women do not "make it," our ideology tells us it is because we are not good enough (men are superior) or we do not try hard enough (it's our fault). The ideology can be so powerful that many women come to define "making it" as getting married — a successful woman is a married woman. Thus, female dependence is guaranteed, and the *status quo* perpetuated. While our ideology is an effective tool in the maintenance of our social order, and serves a male dominated society well, at the same time it ensures the economic vulnerability of women throughout their lives.

The Characteristics of Female Labour Force Participation

It is a well-known fact that female labour force participation rates have increased, particularly over the past 20 years, so that now more than one-half of all women work outside the home. One of the frequently mentioned causes of poverty among today's older women is that a high percentage were full-time homemakers earning no income of their own, making them ineligible for pension benefits (except for widow's benefits in plans carrying such a provision) (Health and Welfare Canada 1982b). While we lack data on the actual numbers of today's elderly women who never worked outside the home,[5] everyday observation informs us that the percentage is higher than it will be for future cohorts. Thus, there is a certain validity in pointing to women's lack of labour force participation as a factor leading to poverty in later life for today's elderly women. Yet the characteristics and conditions of female employment at the present time suggest that increased labour force participation will not, in itself, ameliorate poverty among older women in the future.

To see why this is so, female employment will now be examined. But before doing so, a caution is in order. We simply do not know very much about the characteristics of female employment from a longitudinal perspective. We cannot, for example, focus on today's seventy-five-year old women and describe the patterning and sequencing of their work histories. The best that we can do is to provide an examination of the current situation of female labour. In so doing, we recognize that some progress has been made, and that our data represent an improved situation compared to the experience of older women today.

One of the most striking characteristics of female labour is the degree to which it is segregated. In terms of industries, women are concentrated (defined as constituting 60 percent or more of the labour force) in private household work (95.5 percent in 1982), in hospitals, mainly as nurses and other support staff (78.8 percent), in doctors' offices (71.2 percent), in personal service (61.0 percent), and in finance (60.6 percent). Also, within industries, there is a concentration of women within certain categories. For instance, while women constitute a relatively small portion (36 percent) of the labour force within non-durable manufacturing, they are highly concentrated in the clothing (76.2 percent) and knitting (66.7 percent) industries. In terms of occupation, women are highly concentrated in clerical work. Over 78 percent of clerical workers are women, and women make up nearly 93 per cent of the clerical workers in the finance industry. Overall, women are concentrated in clerical, sales, and service occupations (Armstrong 1984). Such industrial/occupational segregation has important implications for the present and future economic situation of women.

The dual economy theory, representative of a conflict perspective, can be applied to women's segregated employment, although it was not specifically designed with women in mind (Dowd 1980). This theory stresses the fact that Western societies in the twentieth century have experienced a transition from competitive capitalism, a system of small and numerous firms, to monopoly capitalism, a system dominated by a fewer number of large corporations. However, this transition has not occurred equally in all industries — monopoly capitalism is more evident in durable manufacturing and the construction and extraction industries, and is less evident in non-durable manufacturing, agriculture, and retail trade. A resulting dual economy has emerged — the "core" sector of monopoly capitalism and the "peripheral" sector of competitive capitalism.

These sectors differ in two important ways. First, the industries in the core sector are large, unionized, and profitable; hence, their workers make high salaries and have numerous benefits, such as private pension plans. The industries in the periphery are smaller, non-unionized and less profitable; their workers make low wages and do not have pension benefits. Second, the composition of the sectors differs. While men tend to be disproportionately found in the the core industries, women, particularly older women, and minorities are disproportionately represented in the periphery industries.

The fact that women are segregated into jobs in the periphery sector affects their income throughout their life-course: while in the traditionally defined wage-earner ages, they make less money; in old age, they are not likely to receive private pension benefits. Women's poverty, then, is due to structural, rather than individual, factors.

Another important characteristic of women's employment is the preponderance of part-time work.[6] Women constitute 72 percent of all part-time workers in Canada. Of all women in the labour force in 1984, 25.9 percent were employed in part-time work. The comparable figure for men was 7.7 percent (Labour Canada 1986).

Two characteristics of part-time work are important for our purposes here. First, part-time work is paid at a lower wage scale than full-time work. In 1981 dollars, part-time jobs paid an average hourly rate of $6.84 whereas full-time jobs paid $8.64 (Labour Canada 1983). This is partly due to the fact that part-time jobs are heavily concentrated in the lower-paid service sector. Second, part-time work usually does not carry fringe benefits such as private pensions, and part-time work of less than ten hours per week is ineligible for Canada Pension Plan benefits (Labour Canada 1983).

The concentration of women in part-time work has social causes and social consequences. In terms of causation, it is well established that most women work out of financial necessity (not for extra "pin money") and find themselves in part-time employment for two basic reasons. One is society's expectations that women's primary responsibility is domestic — housework and child-rearing. Meissner *et al.* (1975) argue that one way that women *accommodate* themselves to the gender-based division of labour within the household (that is, the household tasks to which men make a minor contribution) is by working fewer hours in the paid labour force. A second reason is that women are unable to find full-time work. The consequences are that women's incomes are low (due to the combined effects of fewer hours worked and the lower hourly wages of part-time work), and their retirement incomes will be low due to poor pension coverage.

Another feature of female employment that has important implications is its non-continuous character. With skyrocketing rates of female labour force participation, it is easy to make the inference that women's employment patterns are approximating men's — that is, that a large proportion of women enters the full-time labour force and remains in it, more or less continuously, until retirement. Such an inference is based on an extrapolation of cross-sectional data which fails to distinguish between intermittent and continuous involvement in the labour force, and is incorrect. Moen (1985), using American longitudinal data covering the period 1972–77 found that only 23 percent of women displayed continuous full-time employment. A greater percentage (30 percent) did not work at all over the period. Among the remainder, combinations of full-time and part-time work, as well as periods out of the labour force, were common. Moen relates the non-continuous character of women's outside-the-home employment to family events and obligations. Women are in and out of the labour force depending upon the needs of their children and aged parents, the vagaries of their husband's job location, etc. As well, women are often in less secure jobs and get laid off (Connelly 1978). As a result, women's life-time earnings are reduced, as is the likelihood of their accumulating pension benefits.

As a combined result of the factors we have discussed — gender segregation in the labour force, the high incidence of part-time employment among women, and the non-continuous work histories of women — women's salaries are substantially lower than men's. At least two of these factors (part-time work and non-continuous employment) can be directly related to women's familial and household responsibilities. A circularity develops: because women earn less than their husbands, they lack bargaining power in terms of the allocation of household work (Veevers 1986); because women bear the brunt of household responsibilities, they are not able to equal men's earning capacity.

It is obvious, then, that women's economic vulnerability is a life-long phenomenon. Poverty among older women becomes acute as their husbands die, and their personal poverty becomes evident. In a similar vein, upon divorce, the standard of living of women, regardless of age, drops by more than one-half.

Attempts to rectify the problem of poverty among women in later life have focussed upon pension reform. We will now turn to proposals aimed at reforming our pension system, particularly for women, and then evaluate their likely effectiveness in lifting older women of today and tomorrow out of poverty.

PENSION REFORM

Canada's pension system is a three-tiered one. The first tier (the public pension programmes) consists of the universal Old Age Security Pension (OAS) (which may be supplemented by a means-tested federal Guaranteed Income Supplement (GIS) and various provincial supplements), and the earnings-related Canada/Quebec Pension Plan (CPP/QPP). The second tier consists of private, employer-sponsored pension plans. The third tier is comprised of private savings programmes such as Registered Retirement Savings Plans (RRSPs), investments, etc. that individuals arrange for themselves.

The major proposals for reform centre on the CPP/QPP, private pension plans, and the possibility of a homemaker's pension. In terms of the CPP/QPP, the following major changes are proposed in the federal Green Paper:

— the implementation of a childrearing "drop-out" provision, which would enable a mother to stay at home to raise children under the age of seven without losing CPP credits;

— increasing the maximum earnings covered more quickly than currently legislated to the level of the average industrial wage;

— the splitting of pension credits, assigning half of each spouse's pension credits to the other spouse;

— a life-time continuing pension equal to 60 percent of a deceased spouse's retirement pension after the benefits had been split (this would result in a pension equal to 80 percent of previous combined CPP income) (Health and Welfare Canada 1982b).

In terms of private pension plans, the following major changes are proposed in the federal Green Paper:

— the vesting of pension credits after two years, *i.e.*, after two years, employees are entitled to benefits from employer contributions as well as their own;

— the transferability or "portability" of pension credits from job to job;

— the splitting of pension credits between spouses in the event of marriage breakdown;
— inflation protection or "indexing;"
— the payment of retirement/survivor benefits over the lives of both spouses;
— the extension of pension coverage to regular part-time workers working for employers with pension plans (Health and Welfare Canada 1982b).

A pension for homemakers is also being proposed. The basic idea is that contributions to the CPP/QPP be made directly by homemakers or on their behalf. One specific suggestion is that mandatory contributions based on one-half the average industrial wage be paid by the husband. For women without husbands, an equivalent amount would be contributed by the state.

The implementation of these proposals is problematic, although some have been enacted: *e.g.*, the childrearing "drop-out" provision of the CPP/QPP; some private plans have liberalized their vesting and portability provisions. In contrast, a homemakers' pension seems quite remote at this time. Our reading of federal government sentiment is that the pension-splitting proposals for the public and private pension plans, the proposal to spread retirement benefits of private plans over the lives of both spouses and the restructuring of CPP/QPP benefits should provide homemakers with adequate income in later life without giving them a pension of their own. However, the province of Saskatchewan, in June 1986, announced its intention to implement a homemaker's pension. The plan will be voluntary, with $300 per year contributed by the homemaker with matching funds provided by the provincial government. In the event of divorce or early widowhood, only those women who could afford to make contributions on their own behalf would have continuous coverage. This programme extends not only to homemakers, but to employed women and men who are not covered by private pension plans.

One of the major difficulties in implementing the federally based proposals is the diversity of branches of government involved in public pension provisions (*e.g.*, Health and Welfare, Veterans Affairs, Finance, the Treasury Board); co-ordinating their efforts is not an easy task (Herzog 1986). A second problem concerns cost. It has been estimated that the proposed CCP/QPP reforms would add costs of another 0.7 percent of total labour force income, over and above the costs required to finance the plans as they stand now. Reforms of the employer-sponsored pension system would probably involve cost increases of 1.5–2.5 percent of the covered payroll (Health and Welfare Canada 1982a).

Let us, for the moment, disregard these difficulties, and assume that the pension reforms we have listed were implemented. Would they substantially increase the income of women in later life, now and in the future? Our assessment is that they would help, but would *not* make the significant impact that we are led to believe. The following reasons are given for our reservations.

First, many of the proposed reforms are focussed upon the private, employer-sponsored plans. However, only about 38 percent of the non-self-employed female labour force is currently covered by such plans (Labour Canada 1986), the result of many of the factors we have already discussed such as the location of women in the periphery sector and the high level of part-time employment among women. Thus, the vesting, indexing and portability reforms would affect only a small percentage of women. Approximately 54 percent of the non-self-employed male labour force is covered by private pension plans (Labour Canada 1986). Thus, a large percentage of women is married to men with no private pension coverage. The reforms related to splitting of pension credits and survivor benefits, then, would clearly not benefit all, or anything approaching all, women. Lastly the provision of extending pension coverage to regular part-time employees working for employers with pension plans is limited in that most part-time work is in the periphery sector which is characterized by a lack of private pension coverage.

Reforms to the CPP/QPP have somewhat more potential for lifting older women out of the poverty state, particularly the reforms related to the splitting of pension credits and survivor's benefits. The homemaker's pension, which would be encompassed under the CPP/QPP, also has the potential for increasing the income of older women. However, it must be remembered that CPP/QPP is designed to replace 25 percent of one's earlier income, with the expectation that the remaining 75 percent comes from private pensions, investments, RRSPs, etc. As Neysmith (1984) points out, this expectation is not tenable for the majority of women.

In terms of the Saskatchewan government's proposed "homemaker's" pension, a major problem comes to mind: its voluntary nature. Women who do not have the financial resources to contribute to the plan are excluded; and they are the very women in most need of pension coverage in old age. Also, the proposed plan contains the potential for increasing women's economic dependence on their husbands. On the other hand, the plan holds considerable promise for increasing the later-life income of employed women (and men). So, in a rather paradoxical way, what is termed a "homemaker's" pension may be of more benefit to women who are not full-time homemakers. While we do not want to discount the importance of increased pension income for these women, it still leaves us with the problem of old-age financial insecurity for that portion of homemakers unable to contribute to the plan.

POLICY IMPLICATIONS

At the present time, more than 50 percent of Canadian women over the age of 65 receive GIS and provincial supplements in addition to OAS. As we have seen, these sources do not total an income that reaches the poverty line for substantial numbers of widows and other non-married women. Poverty does not occur because women become old. As so aptly put by Neysmith (1984), older women are like perennial plants — the roots of their poverty develop earlier in life and come to fruition when they are old.

Policy aimed at ameliorating poverty among women in later life has focussed upon pension reform. But, as we have argued, pension reform, although needed, is not enough. It has focussed largely on changes in the CPP/QPP and private pensions. However, as we have seen, the CPP/QPP is designed to replace only 25 percent of earlier income, and private pensions are, in many cases, not available to women.

More radical changes are needed. Some have argued that the private pension system be abolished, in that it serves the investment capital needs of corporations rather than the welfare needs of individuals (Myles 1982; Neysmith 1984), and that a guaranteed annual income be implemented, regardless of age. While this is one option, our opinion is that such change is not likely in the foreseeable future.

From our perspective, the problem of poverty among women in old age will be alleviated by two measures, operating in concert. First, the pension reforms discussed should be implemented. However, the more basic problem is women's status in the labour force and in the wider society. Intense efforts must be made to equalize the status of women and men at all ages. Such efforts would include: equal pay for work of equal value; the gender de-segregation of the labour force; and equal sharing between spouses in household labour and childrearing. Specific policies that could be implemented include affordable day-care, an intensification of affirmative action programmes, paid paternity leave, bonuses to employers for hiring women in non-traditional jobs, and public education programmes focussing on the social benefits of gender equality. However, implementing change is extremely difficult, as women's inequality is a deeply-ingrained component of our society and of our cultural (ideological) belief system. However, it is in these areas that change must come, for they are the basic causes of women's poverty at all ages. Poverty among older women is simply the cumulated result of gender inequality in the labour force and in society generally.

The economic situation for future cohorts of elderly women depends upon changes in the status of women in general. If equality is achieved, future cohorts of elderly women will be much better off. On the other hand, if women continue to earn less than men, to have interrupted work careers, and to work in the periphery sector of the economy, they will continue to be poor in old age. Women who are never-married and/or childless may be at a slight advantage in old age as they will likely have more continuous job histories, but they will still earn less than men, be less likely to have a private pension, and have less money for savings.

NOTES

1. The 58.5 percent figure (called the 1978 base income cut-off) represents a revision over earlier estimates (the 1969 base) that used 62 percent as the cut-off figure.
2. This figure represents a mid-range value, between $6,877 for rural areas and $9,451 for urban areas with 500,000 or more population.
3. In 1983, four provinces (Newfoundland, Prince Edward Island, New Brunswick, and Quebec) did not provide supplements. In the other provinces and territories, the amount of the supplement varied from $1,200 (for a single person) and $2,400 (for a couple) in the Yukon to $188 (for a single person) and $405 (for a couple) in Manitoba. (National Council of Welfare 1984b).
4. While we recognize that not all individual men exercise power in the wider society, it is nevertheless true that "men" as a category control and dominate our society.
5. The 1984 Statistics Canada Family History Survey, which contains information on the work histories of both women and men, did not interview persons over the age of 65.
6. Labour Canada (1983) contains a discussion of the numerous definitions of part-time work. The most common definition is that part-time employees are persons who usually work less than 30 hours per week, excluding those who work less than 30 hours per week but consider themselves to be full-time workers (*e.g.*, airline pilots).

CHAPTER 5

THE OCCUPATIONAL LIFE-COURSE OF WOMEN

Until recently, researchers have assumed that women's employment outside the home was secondary to their interests concerning home and family. As a result, relatively little attention has been paid to women's experience of work outside the home. In view of the importance paid employment plays in women's lives, we have chosen to examine occupational and family life-course[1] issues separately, in this chapter and the next. We realize that the separation we have introduced here does not exist in the lives of women. Women continue to have the primary responsibility for family concerns while in the labour force, and there is much overlap and interaction between the two spheres. Throughout a woman's adult life-course, she must balance employment and family roles. Choices in either sphere are influenced by constraints in the other.

What becomes evident as one examines the research is that women's outside-the-home work has not been studied in anywhere near the detail that men's work has been (Perun and Bielby 1981). As we shall see, the underlying assumption of much of the research that has been done is that employment will be a problem for women in the form of role conflicts and role overload. That is, the focus is on how employment and family roles interfere with each other. Almost nothing is known about how women make employment choices, what they like about their work, or why they change jobs. Also, comparatively little is known about women's work outside the home that is unpaid (*i.e.*, voluntary work), presumably because it is unpaid and, therefore, like housework, assumed to be not "real" work. Furthermore, as can be seen from the relative lengths of this chapter and the next, there simply is less research (and less Canadian research) on women's employment roles than on women's family roles.

WOMEN'S COMMITMENT TO WORK

It is typically assumed that because women do not work outside the home as continuously as men throughout their adult lives, they are not as committed to their jobs. However, some interesting recent work calls this assumption into question. Women do interrupt their work careers when they have young children at home and, to a lesser extent, in middle-age to care for an elderly parent (Bielby and Bielby 1984; Keating and Jeffrey 1983; Wilson *et al.* 1982). Both of these patterns are more common for middle-class women who can afford to leave the labour force for periods of time than they are for working-class women. However, Bielby and Bielby (1984) found that while becoming a mother significantly reduces young women's labour force participation, it does not reduce women's work commitment, as measured by ratings of career importance, satisfaction expected from career and other aspects of life, expectations about future employment and the importance of future employment. In a similar vein, in a study of retired women, Atchley (1976a) found that work orientation is unrelated to length of time women had worked, their marital status, or the length of time they had been retired. He concludes that once a woman has developed a high work commitment, it is not easily given up. Women express high work commitment (Atchley and Corbett 1977), often as high as men in similar occupational groups (Atchley 1976b), and express relatively low levels of dissatisfaction with their work (Laurence 1961).

Women's high expressed work commitment must be viewed in the light of the discouragement women face in expressing such commitment. There is usually a qualifier attached to women's work commitment. It is "acceptable" to work as long as the commitment is not to the exclusion of family activities (Atchley and Corbett 1977), does not interfere with the married couple's life-style too much (Kimball 1979), and does not involve a strong emotional commitment (Rubin 1979). In short, it is not socially desirable for a woman to express a strong job or career commitment without, at the same time, expressing her concern for her family and/or identifying herself in terms of feminine characteristics such as caring and nurturance (Rubin 1979). Birnbaum (1975) found that married professional women who are very active and successful in their careers all identify their husbands as more brilliant and successful than they are. Kimball (1979) found that among middle-aged middle-class women who were returning to work or school, there was a strong relationship between their commitment, as measured by the certainty of their plans, and the emotional support they received from family and friends.

THE ROLE OF EMPLOYMENT IN WOMEN'S LIVES

Research concerning the relationship between paid employment and women's lives has focussed on four areas: the relative happiness of employed women compared to homemakers; how the kind of work women do influences their satisfaction and well-being; multiple-role strain; and retirement. We will examine the first three topics in this section. Retirement will be considered separately in a section following a brief discussion of unpaid work.

Are employed women or housewives happier? Before answering this question, it is important to consider that housewives are expected to be happy, as they are fulfilling the role that has been presented to women as most important for their satisfaction. Employment for women, on the other hand, is often assumed to involve sacrifice, personal cost, and for married women, role conflict and role overload. Thus, one might expect women to respond to these expectations when asked to rate how happy or satisfied they are. Ferree (1984) found that housewives who score high on social desirability measures (*i.e.*, viewing conforming to social norms as positive) report themselves as happier, more satisfied with life, having more rewarding lives, and being more satisfied with being a homemaker. For employed women, social desirability is not associated with satisfaction measures. In spite of these differences in response style, housewives and employed women overall are not different in ratings of happiness and life satisfaction (Black and Hill 1984; Ferree 1984).

What is clear, however, is that while employed women may not be happier, they are higher in self-esteem, *i.e.*, in thinking of themselves as competent and valuable people (Baruch *et. al.*, 1983; Birnbaum 1975; Coleman and Antonucci 1983), and see their lives as more rewarding (Ferree 1984). Why does this difference exist? One explanation is that housewives have only one major role while employed women usually have more than one. Women with more than one role have an "escape valve:" if things are going badly in one area of life, there is another area in which they can feel better about themselves. For housewives, however, everything depends on how they feel about themselves in relation to their work at home. However, a problem with the "one-role explanation" of why housewives have lower self-esteem is that single employed women have higher self-esteem, like married employed women, even though they, like the housewife, have fewer roles (Baruch *et. al*, 1983; Birnbaum 1975). It may be that in a society that values money and independence, it is easier to feel good about oneself if one has both than if one does not.

Baruch and her colleagues (1983) found that housewives' sense of well-being is very strongly related to their perception of the balance between the positive and negative aspects of homemaking. That is, these women's ratings of both pleasure (happiness, life satisfaction) and mastery (self-esteem) are more dependent on feeling good about their work than is the case for women who are employed. In fact, being employed when one prefers to be at home has no impact on well-being but being at home when one prefers to be employed has a significant depressing effect on well-being. The importance of women's compatibility with homemaking for well-being is supported in a longitudinal study of housewives. Livson (1981) found that among healthy fifty year-old women, those who had personality characteristics incompatible with traditional women's roles had lower psychological health ratings than women with traditional characteristics at age forty.

However, by the age of fifty, the non-traditional women had gained in psychological health. This finding indicates that although homemaking may have a negative impact on psychological health for some women at some points in life, changes are also possible.

How does the kind of job women have effect their life satisfaction? Not surprisingly, a professional job is more satisfying than a non-professional one. Studying middle-aged professional men and women, Sekaran (1986) found they do not differ from each other in job satisfaction, life satisfaction, self-esteem, and career salience, and both groups score higher than non-professional women and men. Older professional women have higher job commitment and rate work as more important than do older non-professional women (Atchley 1976a; Price-Bonham and Johnson 1982). Lovell-Troy (1983) found that prestige of the woman's own job, or in the case of the housewife, her former job, is a much more significant predictor of anomia (a sense that no one cares and that the individual has no influence in society) than is the prestige of her husband's job.

Baruch and her colleagues (1983) found the same overall result as the above studies (*i.e.*, women with higher prestige jobs feel higher mastery), but they also found interesting differences among women in different situations. Among single women, job prestige is critical and influences not only mastery but also pleasure. For no other group does job prestige affect pleasure ratings. In contrast, among divorced women, prestige of job is less related to mastery than for any other group. For single women who have always supported themselves, the kind of job plays a major role in self-perception and satisfaction. On the other hand, for divorced women, who have suffered a large drop in income and may be supporting themselves and their family for the first time, having any job is related to feelings of competence and self-esteem.

Given that women work in the home whether they are also employed outside the home or not, married women who are employed have two jobs. As a result, they have less leisure time than their husbands or than housewives (Cherpas 1985; Hendricks 1977; Luxton 1981; McPherson 1985; Meissner *et. al.* 1975). Women also report feeling more multiple-role strain than men (Sekaran 1986). How serious is multiple-role strain and how does it affect women's lives? To the extent that it is important, it appears to affect working-class women or women with lower prestige jobs more negatively than middle-class women. Ferree (1984) found that working-class employed women's life satisfaction and happiness are negatively related to their feeling rushed. For middle-class employed women, these factors are not related. Sekaran (1986) found that while ratings of multiple-role strain are negatively related to job satisfaction for employed women, this relationship is stronger for non-professional than for professional women. In a study of risk of cardiac heart disease, Haynes and Feinleib (1980) reported that employed women as a group are not at higher risk for heart disease than housewives. However, one group of employed women — clerical workers — is at increased risk, especially if they have children and are married to blue-collar workers. This group is more than three times as likely to suffer cardiac heart disease as non-clerical mothers.

For middle-class women, in particular housewives, having too little to do, rather than too much, appears to be related to low well-being. Ferree (1984) found that feeling rushed is positively correlated to happiness and a rewarding life for middle-class housewives. Similarly, Baruch and her colleagues (1983), in a study of middle-class women, found the highest sense of well-being among married mothers employed in high prestige jobs — just the women who are expected to suffer the most from multiple-role strain. In explaining their results, these authors discuss roles in terms of the rewards they offer women as well as the strains. They propose that it is the balance between rewards and strains that may relate to well-being rather than the number of roles *per se*. This may also help explain why multiple-role strain has more severe effects for women with low prestige jobs. For these women, a combination of low income and lack of variety, interest, and power on the job may well mean that the strains of the added role outweigh the rewards. As well, the lower income of these women means that they have fewer options for reducing the stresses of their role in the home.

VOLUNTARY WORK

While research on the occupational life-course has focussed primarily on paid employment, it is important to keep in mind that volunteering is also work, albeit unpaid labour. Volunteering has been defined in two different ways. One way defines it as unpaid work performed for a formal organization or voluntary association; the other defines voluntary work more broadly, including both formal activities and informal acts such as helping friends, neighbours, and family members. Either way, this issue is of particular importance when considering the lives of women, for volunteers are disproportionatley likely to be women, and their contribution to the wider society is often overlooked. The discussion here focusses upon formal voluntary work; the more informal work that women perform is discussed in the following chapter.

For individuals at all stages of the life-course, the variables of gender, income, and education are important predictors of voluntary activity (Chambre 1984). In other words, volunteers are most likely to be middle-class women. Age is also important; persons under the age of 60 are more likely to be engaged in formal volunteer work than those over the age of 60 (Chambre 1984). This finding is not surprising, as advancing age brings with it failing health and, particularly for women, added care-giving to frail family members, particularly husbands. Research findings suggest that volunteering is an activity that individuals establish quite early in life; it is not adopted later in life to compensate for lost roles. As stated by Chambre (1984, 297) elderly volunteers are "volunteers who became elderly."

Volunteerism among women has undergone important changes in recent years (Nemschoff 1981). Whereas in the past female volunteers were largely homemakers, now volunteers who hold full-time paid jobs outnumber homemakers (although homemakers remain a large part of the volunteer population). Also, it is reported that today's volunteers are more likely to be motivated by self-interest than by self-sacrifice (Nemschoff 1981). For example, women are likely at the present time to volunteer for job-related reasons such as gaining work experience and references and for personal reasons such as meeting people or to help during periods of difficult life transitions such as divorce or widowhood.

It is generally found that older volunteers have higher levels of life satisfaction than their non-volunteering peers. However, a number of different explanations for this finding are possible (Bond 1982). First, it is possible that it is the higher activity levels of volunteers, not the voluntary dimension itself, that leads to higher satisfaction. Second, it may be that people with higher levels of life satisfaction are more likely to serve as volunteers. Third, it could be that through volunteering, life satisfaction is enhanced.

WOMEN'S EXPERIENCE OF RETIREMENT

Early research on retirement assumed generally that the work role was not central to women and, thus, retirement would be easier for them as they were losing a secondary, rather than a primary, role (Gratton and Haug 1983; Palmore 1965; Szinovacz 1983). As Szinovacz (1983) points out, this assumption overlooks single women who are heads of households, career women with a major interest in work, middle-aged women who have returned to work, and men who do not attach primary importance to their work role. On the other hand, Connidis (1982) argues that employed women's greater involvement in family concerns throughout their adult life may allow them to reap greater rewards in retirement through higher quality relationships with children and other kin.

More recent research has focussed on working women's attitudes to retirement, retirement decisions and planning, and adjustment to retirement. Studies indicate that employed women are generally more negative than men about retirement in Canada (Matthews and Tindale 1987) and in the U.S. (Gratton and Haug 1983; Jacobson 1974; Newman *et al.* 1982). Sex differences in attitudes toward retirement are probably less important than the type of job or profession. In a study of lawyers, social workers, high school teachers, and college professors, Kilty and Behling (1985) found that differences among the professions explain retirement attitudes much more than either age or sex. Furthermore, results are mixed as to whether job status makes a difference in attitude toward retirement among women.

Prentis (1980) found professional workers look forward to retirement less than office workers. Price-Bonham and Johnson (1982), on the other hand, found no difference between professional and non-professional employed women in attitude toward retirement. They did find, however, that professional women's attitudes are predicted more by work factors while non-professional women's attitudes are predicted more by financial considerations.

When women *plan* to retire is based largely on financial factors which consist primarily on their own, or in the case of married women, their own as well as their husband's, pension eligibility (Atchley 1982; Gigy 1985–86; Prentis 1980; Shaw 1984). Atchley (1982) found that women more than men plan to retire before they are aged 60, after they are aged 70, or never to retire. Women who plan to retire before the age of 60 are of high socio-economic status, married, and in good health. The women who plan not to retire or to retire after the age of 70 are of low socio-economic status and single. The latter group of women most likely does not have pensions of their own and cannot count on a husband's pension for income.

Do married women plan to retire when their husbands do? The majority of married women does not plan to retire when their husbands do. In one study, only 30 percent of the women plan to retire with their husbands; the strongest predictor of their retirement plans is their own pension eligibility (Shaw 1984). Professional women are less likely than non-professional women to say they will retire at the same time as their husbands (Prentis 1980). Women who are the same age as their husbands are much more likely to plan to retire with their husbands than are women who are either younger or older (Shaw 1984).

When women actually retire is less easily predicted. However, pension eligibility is one of the most important factors. In a U.S. study from the Longitudinal Retirement History Survey which included only single and previously married women, O'Rand and Henretta (1982) found that mothers who entered the labour force after the age of 35 are significantly less likely to be covered by a private pension and are also less likely to retire before the age of 65. Having pension coverage or widowed status increases the probability of women retiring before the age of 65. In a study of widow's labour force participation, Morgan (1984) found that among widowed women over the age of 50, 11 percent of those who were working stopped when their husband died. Although the women were not asked why they stopped working, presumably at least some of those over the age of 60 retired because of eligibility for widow's benefits. In another analysis of the unmarried women in the Retirement History Survey, George *et al.* (1984) found that education, occupation, income adequacy, and pension availability are all significantly correlated with women's retirement. However, when all factors are entered into a multiple regression, only age remains significant, *i.e.*, the older the woman, the more likely she is to be retired. These same authors also examimed the Duke longitudinal sample, which included married women, and again found that only age predicts women's retirement. In contrast, a number of health and income-related factors predict men's retirement independent of age. These findings imply one of two possibilities. The first is that factors that influence women's retirement, such as pension eligibility, may be more highly age-dependent for women than for men. The second is that the studies fail to include factors that are important in women's retirement decisions.

These authors, as well as others (e.g., Gratton and Haug 1983), point out the need for more information on women's retirement decisions. While pension eligibility is undoubtedly important in women's retirement decisions, health, which is an important influence in men's decisions, does not appear to be an important factor for women. However, a recent Canadian study (Matthews and Tindale 1987) reports no difference between women and men in retiring for health reasons. Also, it is probable that family considerations influence women's retirement decisions more than men's. For example, having a dependent in the home increases the husband's but decreases the wife's labour force particpation at retirement age (Gratton and Haug 1983). Also, Canadian women are more likely than men to retire for reasons of ill health of spouse or other family members (Matthews and Tindale 1987).

How do women plan for retirement? Szinovacz (1982b) found that 63 percent of women had made financial plans and 59 percent had made plans concerning hobbies and activities. Financial plans are almost always carried out, while plans for activities and hobbies often are not. In a comparison of male and female retirees in the merchandising industry, Kroeger (1982) found that when formal retirement planning services are available from the employer or the union, women are more likely to use them. However, among those without formal sources, men are more likely to seek out informal sources. Since only 36 percent of the women had worked in settings with formal pre-retirement programmes, their lack of use of informal sources means they are much less likely to prepare for retirement than men.

Both women and men adapt quite well to retirement. In fact, people are often more satisfied with retirement after they retire than they thought they would be before retirement (Atchley 1982; Jewson 1982). There are many styles of retirement and adjustment. In a descriptive study of professional and non-professional women and men, Hornstein and Wapner (1985) found four different styles: 1) transition to old age, in which the person leaves work behind, slows down, relaxes and reflects on his/her life; 2) new beginning, in which the person begins new interests, lives for his/her own needs, gains new energy and denies aging; 3) continuation, in which the person treats retirement as a non-event and continues with work or some other central activity; and 4) imposed disruption, in which the person has not chosen retirement, feels that the loss of work cannot be replaced, and is frustrated.

In a study of retired university employees, women reported more volunteer work and men more teaching and research activities (Kaye and Monk 1984). The authors interpret this difference as reflecting men's greater interest or opportunity in continuing their work after retirement. However, more of the men in this sample had been professors and the women administrators. In studying women's and men's retirement styles, it is important to examine not only the individuals' motivation but also the constraints they face. The women in this study may have wished to change their focus in retirement, while the men did not. However, it is also possible that both wished to continue with work activities but this opportunity was available only to the men. Thus the women's greater involvement in volunteer work after retirement may have been chosen because a work arena was not available to them and volunteer work allowed them to continue to use the organizing and administrative skills they had used in their prior work. Thus, Kaye and Monk's (1984) interpretation of the gender difference in activities after retirement illustrates how bias may enter into research, in this case an implicitly male view that fails to consider the constraints women face.

One concern about retirement is that it may result in a decrease in the size of the woman's social network. However, research indicates that this is largely an unnecessary concern. Both men and women maintain long-term friendships into retirement (Jewson 1982), and retired women, when compared to employed women or housewives, have similarly sized informal support networks (Depner and Ingersoll 1982; Fox 1977; Keith 1982). However, retired women, in comparison to housewives, tend to belong to more formal organizations (Depner and Ingersoll 1982; Keith 1982). Formal organizations may provide retired women with a sense of continuity with their past work through social contact within a structured situation and the opportunity to exercise work skills.

Although retired women are very satisfied with retirement, some factors affect retirement satisfaction. Good health is conducive to retirement satisfaction (Atchley 1982; Block 1982; Hooker and Ventis 1984; Szinovacz 1982a) and, to a lesser extent, so is income (Atchley 1982; Block 1982; Szinovacz 1982a). Atchley (1982) found that both men and women who lived alone are more satisfied with retirement. Also, pre-retirement planning has been linked with increased satisfaction (Block 1982; Szinovacz 1982b). This last finding is of particular interest because, as we noted, women are more likely to use formal sources and less likely to use informal sources for retirement planning as compared to men (Kroeger 1982).

POLICY IMPLICATIONS

An important issue for women in the labour force is retirement planning. Given women's greater use of formal sources for planning (Kroeger 1982), it is important that employers and unions provide courses and counselling for women to help them with retirement planning. Often women want help with financial planning, including information about pensions and government payments they are entitled to and how to apply for them (Kaye and Monk 1984). Health care costs also are a concern, but this applies more to persons in the United States than in Canada. Planning in terms of housing and social activities is sought less and perhaps best handled by individuals. It might, however, be useful to include information about various levels of institutional care and home-help available. Although women of preretirement age may not have immediate need of this information, they may be married to older men who do, and it may help them in their long-term planning for themselves and their spouses.

NOTES

1. The term life-course is typically used by sociologists and the term lifespan by psychologists. Both terms refer to a longitudinal perspective in which women are studied over a period of time.

CHAPTER 6

THE FAMILY LIFE-COURSE OF WOMEN

In this chapter, we seek to provide an overview of the research literature concerning the family lives of women as they age. Given the primacy of the institution of the family throughout women's lives, a considerable amount of research has been conducted in this area. We divide this research into three major categories. First, we examine historical change in family structure and events, and focus upon change in the timing of family life-course events among Canadian women. Second, we discuss the subjective aspects of family and family-related transitions as they affect middle-aged and older women. Third, we examine family interaction patterns in the lives of older women.

Throughout this chapter, a number of themes will be emphasized: a debunking of several myths about families, family change and women's role in family life; the decreasing primacy of traditional family roles in women's lives; and the subjective contradictions inherent in women's familial roles.

AN HISTORICAL OVERVIEW

Changes in Family Structure and the Occurrence of Women's Family Life Events

A long-standing tenet within the normative sociological perspective, particularly structural-functionalism, was that industrialization and modernization resulted in the destruction of the extended (*i.e.*, multi-generational) family and replaced it with the nuclear (*i.e.*, parents and dependent children only) family as the dominant family structure (*e.g.*, Burgess 1960; Cowgill 1974; Parsons 1942). According to this view, elderly persons who previously had a place in the extended family structure became excluded from the family fold, and this change occurred because it met the needs of modern industrial society. This idea continues to be prevalent in society at large, and we find that many students enter courses with this notion of past family life and familial change.

However, at least for the western world, this tenet is erroneous. In part, it represents what Laslett (1983) terms the "world we have lost" syndrome that idealizes and romanticizes past societies and the family life of earlier eras. The work of family historians and historical demographers provides overwhelming evidence that the extended family structure was *never* common in western society (*e.g.*, Anderson 1971; Back 1974; Demos 1968; Laslett and Wall 1972; van de Walle 1976). Particularly instructive are Laslett's (1985) data which show that in England prior to 1800, 86 percent of married women aged 65 and over lived in their nuclear family. While widows were more likely to live with married children (28 percent), more than one-half lived alone or, more commonly, with persons other than their children (often as lodgers and boarders, or as or with servants). In other words, the social practice of elderly persons living apart from their married children is a long-standing one in western society.

While family structure has undergone no fundamental alteration, being largely nuclear, other dimensions of family life which have an impact on women's lives have changed considerably. One of the most significant changes is the decrease in the number of children that women bear. This trend is important not only in its role as the major determinant of population aging, as discussed in Chapter 2, but also in terms of its potential impact on inter-generational relations and, in particular, support for elderly women with failing health. Older Canadian women in the past, *e.g.*, women born in the mid-1800s, bore approximately five children each; today's older women bore between three and three and one-half children each, on average; old women in the future, *e.g.*, women born in the 1950s, are expected to complete their childbearing years with less than two children per woman (Gee 1986). While it must be kept in mind that higher mortality levels in the past meant that not all children would survive to adulthood, it is nevertheless true that the overall trend is one in which older women have a smaller reservoir of children to draw upon if and when the need arises. This trend will not take on major significance for approximately 30 years. The women who are now approaching old age are the mothers of the "baby boom" generation who bore, on average, more than three children. It is when the large numbers of women who comprise the "baby boom" generation reach old age that the full impact of small family size will be felt, although we are not sure exactly what that impact will be.

Historical analysis of childlessness amongst the ever-married female Canadian population reveals a trend of *declining* childlessness, which is expected to be followed by an upward trend. Approximately 12 to 15 percent of ever-married women born between the mid-1800s and 1920 never bore any children. In contrast, only seven percent of ever-married women born in the early 1930s, women who are now in their early and mid-50s, are childless (Gee 1986). It is difficult to know what percentage of today's younger women will complete their reproductive years childless, but estimates are in the range of 15 to 20 percent (Veevers 1985). These trends are important, given that childlessness is an important predictor of institutionalization in later life (Bachrach 1980). These Canadian trends suggest that in the near future, institutionalization rates may decline, but then increase again when women with a higher incidence of childlessness reach older ages.

Trends in never-marrying closely parallel trends in childlessness. Approximately 11 percent of women born in the nineteenth century never married. A downward trend then occurred such that approximatley six percent of women who are now in their early and mid-50s never married (Gee 1986). It is difficult to predict the percentage of today's younger women who will never make the transition into marriage, but present trends suggest that the figure will exceed six percent. Being never-married, like being childless, is a predictor of institutionalization in later life. Together, the trends in never-marriage and childlessness are suggestive of a decreased, then an increased, rate of institutionalization of women in later life. However, as pointed out by Chappell *et al.* (1986), informal emotional and instrumental support provided by friends is very important and may counteract the predicted trend of increased institutionalization. Improvements in community-based services may have the same effect, but research evidence on this issue is mixed (Chappell *et al.* 1986).

The likelihood of divorce is another area of family life that has undergone change in recent decades. We lack long-term historical data on the incidence of divorce in Canada; however, everyday observation, data on annual divorce rates, and the liberalization of our divorce laws in 1968 all point to an increased incidence of divorce within the Canadian population. Nevertheless, divorce is not nearly as widespread in Canada as in the United States. Data from the 1984 Canada Family History Survey indicate that 9.7 percent of ever-married Canadian women aged 50–64 have experienced one (or more) divorce. There is a higher incidence of divorce among younger women; *e.g.*, 16.1 percent of ever-married women aged 40–49 have been divorced (Burch 1985). Still, these figures are substantially lower than those for the American population.

It is not easy to assess the impact of increased divorce on the lives of older women. Some of the women will remarry; some will enter common-law unions of greater or lesser stability; others will not form another union. For women who do not form a permanent union with another man, the greatest impact will probably be economic. A high risk of poverty or near-poverty throughout the rest of their lives is likely, given the discussion provided in Chapter 4.

Changes in the Timing of Women's Family Life Events

An off-shoot of the age stratification theory within sociology, one of the theories subsumed under the normative perspective discussed in Chapter 1, is the sociology of the life-course. This branch of inquiry is usually referred to as the "life-course perspective" (Elder 1978). It will be noted that the term "perspective" is used, in this case, to refer to a specific focus of study within a given theoretical approach, and thus is a different, more narrow, usage of the term than the one provided in Chapter 1.

Within the life-course perspective, one of the main areas of interest is "social time," or the ordering of events and social roles by age-linked expectations, sanctions, and options (Elder 1978). One of the dimensions of social time concerns social timetables for the occurrence of significant life events or, in other words, transitions to and from major role statuses. Major role transitions related to the family include entering (and exiting from) marriage, birth of the first child, birth of the last child, empty nest, and widowhood.

Here, we will briefly examine data relating to changes in the timing of these family life transitions, and discuss the consequences of these changes for the lives of Canadian women. For the purposes of illustration, we will focus on four cohorts of women only: women born in 1841–50; 1901–10; 1931–40; and 1951–60. Before looking at the data, three cautions are in order. One, some portion of women in each cohort does not experience some or all of the transitions we will be examining. For example, women who are never-married and childless would experience none of these life events. Two, the data for the younger two cohorts, particularly relating to the later life transitions, are estimates only. These women are not old enough to have experienced the complete range of life-course events. Details of the estimation procedures are provided in Gee (1986). Three, these data do not take into account marriage break-up due to divorce.

It can be seen in Table 6.1 that age at first marriage has declined substantially among Canadian women, a trend that is in keeping with the experience of other western societies. Contrary to popular belief, women in past eras did not marry at young ages. Also, the recent trend toward later age at first marriage is quite minor when viewed historically.

Paralleling the declines in age at first marriage is a trend toward younger age at first birth. While there has been a recent upward trend in age at first birth, it is similarly quite small. It only *appears* substantial if we compare women born in the 1950s with women born in the 1930s. However, the cohort of the 1930s was very atypical in terms of timing of life events — this group of women, relatively small in numbers due to the low fertility of the Depression era, married young and had their children young and, as a result, created the "baby boom."

The age at which women bear their last child has declined a considerable amount. Where as women born in the mid-1800s bore their last child at age 40, their counterparts born in the mid-1900s completed childbearing at age 26.3. While decreasing age at marriage is, in part, responsible for this trend, the major factor involved is a decline in the number of children that women bear.

It will be noted that our data concerning the timing of childbearing do not indicate the highly publicized phenomenon of delayed motherhood. While

TABLE 6.1

MEDIAN AGE AT FAMILY LIFE-COURSE EVENTS AND YEARS SPENT IN LIFE STAGES, CANADIAN FEMALE BIRTH COHORTS

	Birth Cohort			
	1841–50	1901–10	1931–40	1951–60
Median age at:				
—first marriage	26.0	23.3	21.1	22.5
—first birth	28.0	25.0	22.9	24.5
—last birth	40.0	29.1	29.1	26.3
—empty nest[a]	60.1	49.1	49.1	46.3
—widowhood	59.5	61.3	67.2	69.9
—death of women	64.3	67.3	79.4	82.2
Years spent:				
—between marriage and first birth	2.0	1.7	1.8	2.0
—raising dependent children	32.1	24.1	26.2	21.8
—married, with no dependent children	−0.6	12.2	18.1	23.6
—in widowhood	4.8	6.0	12.2	12.3

[a] Age of mother when last child is aged 20.

SOURCE: Adapted from Gee (1986).

it is undoubtedly true that *some* women are postponing motherhood, our data indicate that most are not.[1] Today's "postponing" mothers are members of the highly visible, successful middle class. While they get considerable publicity, they are numerically so small that their behaviour does not substantially increase the average age at childbearing.

The median age at widowhood has increased by over ten years for the cohorts represented here. To a small degree, the narrowing of the age difference between husbands and wives accounts for this trend, but the major factor involved is increased longevity.

As a result of these changes in the timing of family life-course events, there has been a fundamental alteration in the number of years that women spend in various life-course stages. The time spent in rearing dependent children has decreased by more than ten years. Women are now free of major childrearing tasks when they are in their mid-40s. In the past, the average woman could expect to be widowed before her last child left home. Now, she can expect nearly 24 years in which she and her husband live together alone before she is widowed. In addition, the years spent as a widow have more than doubled, so that today's women can expect to be widows for more than 12 years.

Taken together, these data point to the declining primacy of traditional familial roles in women's lives. Today's average woman will live 60 years after marrying. Of these 60 years, 40.2 years (67 percent) will be spent without major childrearing responsibilities, and 12.3 years (21 percent) will be spent without a spouse (assuming no divorce takes place). In contrast, her counterpart born in the mid-1800s would have only 6.2 years (16 percent) of life after marriage without childrearing tasks, and 4.8 years (12.5 percent) spouseless.

The cornerstones of the traditional female role in our society are "mothering" and "wifing." These activities are taking up an increasingly smaller portion of women's lives. Inter-related with this change is increased female labour force participation (which can be viewed as both cause and consequence of these family life-course changes) and increased divorce (which, in all seriousness, can be viewed, at least in part, as a consequence of the decreased likelihood of widowhood at younger ages).

At the same time, other familial roles for women have gained in importance, largely as a function of increasing longevity and, secondarily, as a result of a decreasing number of years between generations. These "new" roles include the caring for frail, elderly parents and the greater likelihood of experiencing grandmotherhood and great-grandmotherhood.

TRANSITIONS IN WOMEN'S FAMILY LIVES

In this section we examine some of the familial transitions that women experience throughout adulthood, both within and between generations. For two reasons, most of the research discussed examines transitions that married women face. One, most women are married for at least part of their adult lives; and, two, very little research looks at transitions in the lives of single women, perhaps because they experience fewer transitions. However, some of the transitions discussed here, *e.g.*, parent's ill health, are faced by both married and single women. In addition, other transitions, such as empty nest and grandmotherhood, are common to single as well as married mothers. As more married women spend a larger proportion of their adult lives in the paid labour force, issues of combining employment and family responsibilities become increasingly important to them. Although we have chosen to look at family and employment issues in separate chapters, we realize they are not separate in women's lives. Where data are available concerning the interaction of paid employment with family transitions we have included them. As the reader will see in the following sections, we need to know a good deal more about how women's employment interacts with their family responsibilities.

In our examination, we adopt a dialectical perspective that looks at marriage within the wider social, economic, and historical context. A woman's marriage is very different from her husband's marriage in a number of important ways. If she is a housewife, she will be economically dependent and, thus, less free to leave the marriage than he is. Even if she works in the labour force in a full-time job, it is likely that she will earn less than he does, as seen in Chapter 4. If there are children, she will most likely be responsible for them. If the couple divorces, her income will be reduced while her husband's will increase, and she will care for the children, usually with little or no child support. She is more likely to be widowed and remain so but he is more likely to remarry, if widowed or divorced.

Mid-life Transitions[2]

Empty Nest

The empty nest is a twentieth-century phenomenon. In earlier times, women often did not live to see their youngest child leave home. With increasing longevity, the decreasing number of children born to women, and the younger ages at which childbearing is completed, the empty nest has become a focus of researchers.

Is the empty nest a crisis or a relief for middle-aged mothers? The answer depends very much on the sample that is studied. Clinical samples often reveal that women face problems with the empty nest (Bart 1971); normative samples of middle-aged women and cross-sectional studies show that women experience relief and even increased well-being when the youngest child leaves home (Black and Hill 1984; Borland 1982). Rubin (1979) found that most of her sample of middle-class and working-class women report relief. She did find the empty nest is temporarily more difficult for working-class women because they are less able to anticipate when it will occur and to prepare for it. Middle-class women work through issues in anticipation of children going to university; working-class women, on the other hand, deal with the transition after their children leave home. In a larger questionnaire study, Black and Hill (1984) found that empty nest status is related to women's general happiness but that the amount of the variance in happiness explained by empty nest status is so minimal as to be unimportant.

When does the empty nest occur? Most researchers have defined it in terms of when the youngest child graduates from high school.[3] However, when women are asked *their* definitions, answers range from "when the youngest child goes to kindergarten" to "when the youngest child moves out" to "when the youngest child gets married." In one study, only 1.3 percent of women agreed with researchers that the empty nest occurs when the youngest child graduates from high school (Harkins 1978). Women are much more likely to state that the "going away to school" (41.3 percent), "moving out" (39.4 percent), or "getting married" (17.1 percent) of the youngest child is indicative of the empty nest.

Harkins also investigated the relationship between both an objective definition of empty nest (last child graduating from high school) and a subjective definition (mother's own) with physical and psychological well-being. Using the objective definition, women who have recently experienced the empty nest are slightly more likely to report physical symptoms. Using the subjective defintion, the women in transition are slightly more likely to report positive psychological well-being.

For most women, the empty nest transition is a neutral or slightly positive experience. For a small minority of women, it is a crisis. We know very little about the factors that make it a crisis for these women. Being employed is associated with a better adjustment to the empty nest but, again, the variance accounted for is so small that employment cannot be considered a major or even important factor (Black and Hill 1984). Degree of involvement with children (Bart 1971) and ability to cope with, and learn from, change (Black and Hill 1984) may be important factors in whether or not the transition is traumatic.

Caring for Elderly Parents

For many middle-aged, and even elderly, women a significant transition occurs in their lives when they become involved with caring for frail, aging parents. It is estimated that 8 to 10 percent of elderly people living outside of institutions are as impaired as those in institutions and that a further 6 to 7 percent can leave their homes only with difficulty (Brody 1981). For the most part, these people are cared for by women — either their wives or their daughters or daughters-in-law.

Most people feel a strong obligation to care for parents who need financial, social, personal and/or emotional support. There is an age difference in perceived obligation: young people express the strongest sense of filial duty; elderly people, the least (Brody 1981; Storm *et al.* 1985). Middle-aged and elderly women are more likely to prefer support from formal rather than family sources (Brody 1981). In other words, people who are closest to being involved with giving *or* receiving care are more likely to prefer the independence afforded by support services outside the family. This is especially true for financial and personal support and in situations where children are not financially advantaged (Storm *et al.* 1985).

People of all ages expect adult children to provide emotional support to elderly parents (Brody 1981). For this type of support, elderly women expect daughters, especially unmarried daughters, to adjust their work schedules in order to help them more than they expect sons to do so and more than middle-aged women think is appropriate (Brody *et al.* 1984).

Actual care given varies from none or very little in the case of a parent who is healthy and lives independently to what amounts to a full-time job in the case of a bedridden parent who lives in the home of a daughter or daughter-in-law. The biggest factor influencing amount of time spent caring for an elderly mother is whether the mother lives with the daughter. Daughters whose mothers live with them spend an average of 28.5 hours per week in caring for their mothers while daughters whose mothers live independently spend an average of 3.5 hours per week (Lang and Brody

1983). However, a recent Canadian study (Rosenthal 1986b) indicates that it is important to distinguish between multi-generational households located in the child's home and those located in the parents' home. More care is needed if the parent lives in the home of the child. Sons are likely to provide care only in situtations where a daughter is not available. Also, they are more likely to depend upon their spouse for help. However, even when sons provide the same amount of care as daughters, they are less likely than daughters to see negative consequences for themselves (Horowitz 1985). These last two findings are likely related: because sons rely on their wives, at least part of the pressure is relieved for them.

A recent American study (Brody and Schoonover 1986) found no difference between employed and non-employed daughters in the amount of care provided to their disabled, widowed, community-dwelling mothers. Working daughters provided as much affective support and as much instrumental help with such tasks as housework, laundry, grocery shopping and financial management. However, for two types of tasks — meal preparation and personal care — working daughters did less *but* arranged for these services to be provided by others, most often through purchased help. Thus, the trend of increasing female labour force participation does not appear to be leading to reduced care for frail mothers, or to increased use of state-subsidized services. These findings relate to Canadian data that indicate that most services provided to elderly persons are provided informally (Chappell *et al.* 1986; Connidis 1985).

In caring for an elderly parent, considerable stress and conflict may arise which strains affectionate and emotional bonds across generations. Thus, women who are already under considerable pressure may feel guilty as well if they do not feel affectionate toward their parent. Jarrett (1985) proposes that in helping these women, it is important to relabel what they see as a personal problem (I don't love her enough) to a situational problem (emphasizing the time and energy necessary for care-giving) and to point out that it is only recently that affection, rather than obligation, has been assumed to be the "proper"motivation for providing care.

Old-Age Transitions

Grandmotherhood

Becoming a grandmother is a role change that is not well-defined in our society. Although most women describe grandmotherhood as a very significant role and one that gives them much pleasure, actual contact with grandchildren is not as highly related to life satisfaction as is frequency of contact with friends (Wood and Robertson 1978).

Being a grandparent has aspects of both an ascribed and an earned status. One becomes a grandmother when her child has a child. However, it is only through active involvement on the part of the grandmother that the role takes on a personal meaning.

Most studies of grandparenthood have focussed on the symbolic, formal aspects of the role (a concern for doing what is morally right and socially correct with one's grandchildren) and/or the personal, informal aspects of the role (an emphasis on having fun with and indulging grandchildren). The role or combination of roles a grandmother takes on depends not only on her own choice but also on the wider social context in which she becomes a grandmother. For example, she is likely to be closer to her daughter's than her son's children (Fisher 1983; Kahana and Kahana 1971); to be more actively involved with grandchildren who live near her (Fisher 1983) and who are younger (Kahana and Kahana 1971); and to be more involved on a personal, individual level if she is older, unemployed, and has few friends (Robertson 1977).

Grandmothers depend on their adult children for contact with their grandchildren. This point can be illustrated by examing the relationship between grandparent and grandchild when the grandchild's parents divorce (Matthews and Sprey 1984). If the grandparent's child is granted custody, the grandparents are more likely to maintain contact. Since it is mostly mothers who get custody, this means that maternal grandparents are more likely to keep in contact with their grandchildren. However, 47 percent of grandparents remain friendly with their child's former spouse. This feat is accomplished largely through refusing to blame either of the adult children for the divorce and offering needed resources and support. Most of these grandparents name several roles to describe their relationship with their grandchildren, but they are significantly more likely to name surrogate parent than are grandparents whose children are still married.

In summary, there is a wide range of both role definition and behavioural involvement of grandmothers with their grandchildren. Although many, especially younger, more socially involved grandmothers adopt fairly distant, formal and symbolic roles, others become actively involved in their grandchildren's lives. Most often, these activities are short-term ones such as babysitting, visiting, and recreational activities. However, sometimes they involve extended time periods. In one study, 28 percent of grandmothers reported taking their grandchildren on vacation (Robertson 1977). Moreover, some grandmothers become surrogate parents on a part-time or full-time basis.

Caring for Elderly Husbands

Women tend to marry men who are older than they, and, as we have already seen, women outlive men by a number of years. Both of these factors result in a situation in which many elderly women are involved in the care of their husbands. It is estimated that two-thirds of men who are not in institutions, but who are disabled or bedfast, are cared for by their wives (Streib and Beck 1980). For many women this care-giving, while voluntarily provided, results in great strain, particularly as it can coincide with their own failing health and with diminishing financial resources. They are called upon to complete tasks which their husbands formerly performed and with which they may be unfamiliar. Most women do not wish to institutionalize their husbands for personal and, particularly in the United States, financial reasons. These women wish they could get away or have a break and then, like middle-aged women caring for an elderly parent, feel guilty. Also, as with middle-aged caregivers, a recent Canadian study indicates that elderly women caregivers feel more burdened and assess their role more negatively than elderly male caregivers (Marcus and Jaeger 1984). Support services such as support groups of wives also caring for their ailing husbands, respite services, adult daytime care, and home services can make a significant improvement in these women's lives (Crossman *et al.* 1981).

Since so much time can be involved in the care of a disabled spouse, the couple may have little time to continue social contacts. This isolation increases the wife's vulnerability at the same time as the husband becomes increasingly dependent on her. In a study of elderly individuals without children who had just been released from an acute-care hospital, Johnson and Catalano (1981) found that married people are more isolated than single people in terms of contact with relatives, friends, and neighbours.

Widowhood

Widowhood is a women's issue. Because women live longer than men and marry men older than themselves, they are approximately four times more likely to be widowed (Table 6.2). While women are more likely to become widows, they are less likely to remarry. Canadian data indicate that, for all age groups, widowers are four and one-half times more likely to remarry than are widows. Among the population aged 70 and over, widowers are approximately nine times more likely to remarry (Northcott 1984).

With widowhood, women experience a personal loss, an income reduced by as much as half, a disrupted and often reduced social network, and poor health (Barrett 1977). It is generally agreed that widowhood is the most stressful role transition that women experience (Matthews 1986). What kind of support is helpful to a woman facing widowhood? The kind of support needed varies with how recently the woman has been widowed. In the first year, she is engaged in grieving and needs emotional support, nurturance, and comfort. Although the widow is in increased contact with her children, especially her daughters, contact with her own parents (if alive) and widowed and single friends is more beneficial to her morale than contact with her own children (Bankoff 1983). Also, continued emotional contact with her deceased husband may be a significant source of support. Approxi-

TABLE 6.2

WIDOWED POPULATION AGED 55 AND OVER, BY SEX: CANADA, 1981

	Widows		Widowers		
Age	Number	Percent	Number	Percent	Ratio[a]
55–59	79,500	13.0	14,885	2.6	5.3
60–64	109,005	21.1	19,395	4.2	5.6
65–69	142,985	31.5	26,180	6.7	5.7
70–74	155,290	44.1	30,395	10.8	5.1
75–79	145,050	57.5	31,285	17.3	4.6
80–84	113,600	70.2	26,265	27.7	4.3
85–89	68,675	79.0	17,815	40.5	3.9
90+	36,610	84.7	10,880	55.5	3.4

[a] Number of widows divided by number of widowers.

SOURCE: *1981 Census of Canada*, Statistics Canada Catalogue No. 92-901, Table 4.

mately half of widows report talking to, or otherwise experiencing, their deceased husbands as a positive and comforting experience (Barrett 1981).

When a woman has been widowed for more than 18 months, she is past the most intense phase of grief and begins to build a new life for herself. During the next few years and beyond, different sources of support are most closely related to morale. Contact with friends, particularly widowed and single friends, replaces her own parents as the source of support that contributes the most to her sense of well-being (Bankoff 1983). Contact with her children continues to be a less important contributor to her well-being than contact with friends and neighbours (Arling 1976; Bankoff 1983). Also, Canadian studies (*e.g.* Matthews 1986) indicate that siblings, particularly sisters, are important sources of support for widows. These findings suggest that the impact of smaller family size among future cohorts of widows will be mixed: fewer children may be relatively unimportant but fewer sisters to draw upon may create problems.

One of the most interesting findings to emerge from the studies of widow-hood adjustment and morale is the primary importance of contact with other widows. The importance of parental support may be related to this finding as a middle-aged or elderly widow's living parent, in most cases, will be a widowed mother. Widows report twice as many widowed as married friends (Roberto and Scott 1984–85). Contact with widowed friends is a major predictor of well-being, while contact with married friends has a small but negative impact on well-being (Bankoff 1983). Most intervention programmes promote contact with other widows (Barrett 1978; Silverman and Cooperband 1975). Thus, although widows have contact with children and other family members, it appears to be contact with age peers who share their life experiences that most directly affects their morale in a positive direction.

INTERACTION WITH FAMILY AND FRIENDS

In this section, we focus on two issues related to older women's interactions with family and friends. The first issue concerns the relative importance of the quantity, as opposed to the quality, of social contacts. The second concerns the relative importance of family and friends in the social worlds of older women. Throughout our discussion of the second issue, variations related to women's different life situations (*e.g.*, varying marital statuses) are examined.

Interaction Patterns: Quantity or Quality?

Much of the research concerned with older women's social networks has focussed upon the *amount* of contact women have with family members (in particular, children), neighbours, and friends. While a high percentage of aged women (nearly one-third of Canadian women aged 65 and over in 1981) lives alone (Statistics Canada 1984b), research findings indicate that a preference for privacy and independence is prevalent within the elderly Canadian population (Wister 1985)[4] and that children live near by and frequently visit their parents (*e.g.*, Shanas 1979). In addition, recent research makes clear that *quality* of interpersonal contact is much more critical to older women's sense of well-being or life satisfaction than is the *quantity* of interaction. This important point can be illustrated in four ways.

First, a growing body of research that compares objective measures of social support (number of contacts, frequency of contact, amount of aid given or received) with subjective measures (does the woman have as much contact as she would like?) has shown consistently that objective measures do not relate to measures of well-being or life satisfaction while subjective ones do (Beckman and Houser 1982; Creecy *et al.* 1985; Lee and Ellithorpe 1982; Liang *et al.* 1980; Quinn 1983; Ward *et al.* 1984). Within parent-child relationships, it has been shown that ratings of intimacy or quality of contact are unrelated or only minimally related to frequency of visits, amount of aid given, or frequency of contact (Moss *et al.* 1985; Walker and Thompson 1983).

Most of these studies are based on large-scale probability samples of women and men. Unfortunately, they do not always examine the patterns of relationships separately for women and men; therefore, we cannot be certain the relationships reported apply to women. However, two of the above studies (Beckman and Houser 1982; Walker and Thompson 1983) used all female samples. Also, if the patterns for men and women were very different, it is unlikely that the overall results would reveal such a consistent pattern. Nevertheless, in the future it is important for researchers to check and report on similarities and differences in the relationships for men and women.

Second, the concept of compensation illustrates the importance of quality of contact. It has been proposed that older women who are unmarried and/or have no children and, thus, are deprived of contact with spouse or children compensate by increasing their contact with other family members or friends. Support for the compensation hypothesis is mixed: some studies report no compensation (Babchuck 1978–79; Bachrach 1980); others report compensation for unmarried or single women (Atchley *et al.* 1979; Longino and Lipman 1981). Both of the latter studies found compensation occurs among professional high-income women and it may be that resources help older women increase their social contacts. What is *more* important is that whether single and childless women compensate or not, they are not lower in well-being or life satisfaction than married women or older mothers (Gubrium 1974; Beckman and Houser 1982; Glenn and McLanahan 1981).

Third, the well-established relationship between having a confidant and well-being in old age illustrates the importance of quality of social inter-action. A confidant is a person, who may be either a family member or a friend, in whom the older woman confides her troubles, worries, joys, and embarrassments. In an early study, Lowenthal and Haven (1968) report that having a confidant protects older people against depression in the face of such role losses as widowhood and retirement. The only major change in old age for which a confidant does not provide protection is a serious health problem. Lowenthal and Haven also report that women are more likely to have a confidant than are men, and if they have a confidant it is less likely to be their spouse than is the case for their husbands. These findings have been verified several times since then (*e.g.*, Babchuck 1978–79; Powers and Bultena 1976; Trela and Jackson 1979). The pattern that emerges is that men interact with more people and have more frequent contact with a number of people while women have more intense interaction with more intimate friends (Powers and Bultena 1976).

Fourth, time spent alone is not necessarily related to loneliness, as would be expected if quantity of social interaction were critical to well-being. Even though older single women spend the most time alone and married women the least, they are similar to each other in satisfaction and exhibit higher levels of satisfaction than either divorced or widowed women (Gubrium 1974). Similar findings have been reported in terms of health. Single women are more similar to married women than they are to divorced and widowed women in health status (Verbrugge 1979b). It is a change from married to divorced or widowed status rather than an unmarried status *per se* that results in a decline in perceived health (Fenwick and Burresi 1981).

How much time do older people spend alone and what effect does it have on their mood at the time? In a recent Canadian study (Larson *et al.* 1985), retired, community-living adults wore electronic pagers during the day. They were "beeped" at random intervals: when the beep occurred they recorded information including the time, where they were, if they were alone or not, and their affective, arousal, and cognitive states. Men and women who were married spent 40 percent of their time alone on average; people living with someone else were alone 54 percent of the time; those living alone spent 73 percent of their time alone. More women than men lived alone but there was no sex difference in time spent alone when marital status was controlled.

The authors report that older people do not wish to have constant companionship and do not suffer as much decrement in mood when alone as is the case for younger people. Furthermore, for married people being alone creates a contrast that is energizing and challenging. Being alone has less positive consequences for the unmarried, but this occurs whether they live alone or not.

We have examined four different areas of research that indicate that quantity of social contact has very little bearing on older women's well-being, while quality is quite important. Isolation in old age may be critical not so much when older women have a lowered amount of contact, but when they lose the people, such as confidants, who provide quality contact.

Interaction Patterns: Family or Friends?

Traditionally kin,[5] particularly children, have been assumed to be the main source of support for older women. Friends, however, may be as important or more important than kin, as we observed in our discussion of widows' support networks. In the discussion below, we will examine both familial and friendship relationships as they relate to the quality of older women's lives.

How do older women experience their marriages? In general, people who have been married a long time report quite positive feelings about their marriages. They emphasize expressive qualities such as support, understanding, companionship and the expression of feelings as what they value most in their marriages (Roberts 1980; Stinnett et al. 1972). There is some evidence, however, that marriage may not be as positive for people over the age of 70 as it is for younger elderly people (Gilford 1984). This finding is probably a function of declining resources and health with advancing age. An interesting difference in older women's and men's views of their marriages is that women perceive support within the marriage as less plentiful than do men, for both support received and support given (Depner and Ingersoll-Dayton 1985).

How does divorce affect elderly women? At all ages, women who divorce suffer more economic hardship than men and are less likely to remarry, factors which are often ignored in the research on divorce (Baker 1984). Older women and men experience divorce as more upsetting than younger people. Specifically, they experience greater unhappiness, disruption of their social world, long-term dissatifaction, personal discomfort, pessimism about the future, and uncertainty about what to do next (Chiriboga 1981). Both men and women suffer in divorce, but women are more likely than men to experience a lowered standard of living, psychological symptoms, emotional tension, and personal disorganization (Chiriboga 1981). Divorced women are less likely than divorced men to report dissatisfaction with family life (Uhlenberg and Myers 1981), probably a reflection of their greater contact with kin (Rosenthal 1985) and their lesser reliance solely on their spouse for support.

Some older divorced women remarry, although the likelihood is much less than for men. Successful older marriages are those where the couple has known each other for more than 11 years, has the approval of family and friends, has an adequate income, has high life satisfaction, and where the couple does not live in the previous home of either of the spouses (McKain 1972).

Although we lack good information concerning frequency, a minority of older women lives in either common-law or lesbian relationships. Although common-law unions are a life style more common among younger people (Burch 1985), some older heterosexual people may choose to live together without marrying for financial reasons. Lesbian relationships, especially among older women, are likely to be monogamous, long-term relationships. Fourteen percent of lesbians aged 21 to 25 percent report at least one relationship longer than five years, but 80 percent of those aged 41 to 50 report at least one relationship in excess of five years (Lewis 1979).

In spite of the stereotyped view that children protect against loneliness in old age, having children has very little effect on life satisfaction. Having children has a small but positive effect on family satisfaction (Singh and Williams 1981); a small but negative effect on marital happiness, especially for women (Glenn and McLanahan 1982; Spanier and Lewis, 1980); and little relationship with well-being except for certain sub-groups such as widows, whose well-being is slightly higher if they have children (Beckman and Houser 1982; Glenn and McLanahan 1981). Childless older women are overall as satisfied with their lives as women with children. Furthermore, childless older women are significantly more likely to name advantages to not having children and significantly less likely to name disadvantages than are women with children (Houser *et al.* 1984). However, as noted previously, one way in which having children does affect older women is that they are less likely to live alone or be institutionalized if they have children (Bachrach 1980).

The mother-daughter relationship is one that is particularly enduring and emotionally important. Daughters are more likely to provide aid to their elderly mothers and to have their mothers live with them. Mothers are significantly more likely to name their daughters than their sons as confidants (Aldous *et al.* 1985). Adult middle-aged daughters report quite positive relationships with their mothers and their sense of self-esteem and mastery are positively related to the quality of their relationship with their mothers (Baruch and Barnett 1983). This relationship is particularly strong for married, unemployed daughters who do not have children of their own.

Kin, especially same-generation kin such as sisters, are important to older women, particularly single women. Unmarried or single women sometimes compensate by increasing their contact with secondary kin (Longino and Lipman 1981; Atchley *et al.* 1979). Among older women, single childless women are most likely to live alone, but they also are more likely to live with other relatives than women who have children, somewhat reducing the effect of childlessness on living alone (Bachrach 1980). Marriage can even, in some situations, reduce contact with other kin to the point that ill elderly who are married have fewer kin interactons than single ill elderly (Johnson and Catalano 1981).

Friends may be more important to elderly women than has been previously supposed. Although elderly women tend not to live with non-kin friends, they do have friends in significant numbers, and quality of friendship, particularly confidant relationships, is related to their well-being. In a study of elderly people in Winnipeg (Chappell 1983), it is reported that activities with non-family peers are more satisfying than activities with family. Friends may be particularly valuable sources of support because they share the same generational experiences and the relationships are voluntary rather than obligatory. When a friend helps you, it is clear it is out of a sense of caring or of reciprocity and that you will also help in return. With family, particularly children, the helping may be more one-way.

If friendship is based on an ethic of (approximately) equal exchange, what happens when one person gives more than the other? Two recent studies show that older women who see themselves as over-benefited in their friendships are more distressed and angry, and display lower morale than women who perceive an equal exchange or women who perceive themselves to be under-benefited (Roberto and Scott 1984–85; 1986). It may be that over-benefited older women feel more dependent and less in control than the other women. This finding suggests that being *needed* may be more important to morale in old age than being helped. Friends may be particularly important people not only because we need them but, more importantly, they need us in a way kin, particularly younger kin, do not.

POLICY IMPLICATIONS

A number of policy implications emanate from our review of the family life-course of women. As we have seen, traditional family roles are making up an increasingly smaller portion of women's lives. Clearly, women are "ready" to participate in a fuller way in the broader society. At the same time, their equal participation is blocked by many of the factors discussed in Chapter 4 such as the gender segregation of the labour force, and by the increasing importance of other familial demands, such as the care of ailing parents. In terms of this chapter, policies regarding care-giving are critical.

If women are to be equal members in an aging society, three societal options regarding care-giving are possible: (1) a sharing of care-giving responsibilities between women and men; (2) a higher rate of institutionalization of frail, elderly persons; and (3) increased support for care-giving women. The first option seems very remote, given our society's structural organization and values. The second option is undesirable on both humanitarian and economic grounds. In terms of finances, the costs of home care are only 11 to 14 percent of the costs of institutional care (National Advisory Council on Aging 1986). With increasing numbers and proportions of old people in our society, the costs of a higher level of institutionalization would be great. The third option, although in our opinion less preferable than the first, is the one that is most feasible and likely.

It is clear that caregivers, both middle-aged daughters and elderly wives, need considerably more support than they are now receiving. Help can come in a number of forms. Respite care, in which the caregiver is provided with several days "off," is important. Equally important are adult daytime care and specific home services. In one study (Crossman *et al.* 1981), elderly wives report that having a registered nurse visit and help them for as little as four hours per week makes a significant difference in their ability to care for, and their confidence about caring for, their husbands.

Another area of policy concern is in the design of housing for elderly women. This is particularly important for single and childless women who are more likely to live in an institution. Since we know that quality of interaction is important, housing should be designed to maximize interaction with age peers in a way that allows for the development of confidant relationships, or encourages the continuation of confidant relationships that already exist.

NOTES

1. This conclusion is supported by data from the Canada Fertility Survey which indicate that more than one-half of all first births occur prior to 19 months of the first marriage and only nine percent occur after five years of marriage (Krotki *et al.* 1986).
2. We have divided transitions into "mid-life" and "old-age" for the purposes of discussion. In real life, these transitions are not as clearly associated with age as our division implies. For example, a younger woman

may become a widow; a middle-aged woman a grandmother; or an elderly woman the main source of care for her parents.

3. It will be noted that this definiton contains a middle-class bias. It seems to assume that high school graduation is followed by the child's departure to a college dormitory.

4. A recent Canadian study (Thomas and Wister 1984) indicates that the major predictors of living alone for older women are fertility (*i.e.*, number of children) and ethnicity. In terms of ethnicity, English are more likely to live alone than French, and Jews are more likely to live alone than Italians.

5. We are using the terms "family" and "kin" as synonymous in this section.

CHAPTER 7

THE DOUBLE STANDARD OF AGING: IMAGES AND SEXUALITY

In this chapter we turn our attention to the double standard of aging and evaluate its effect on women's perceptions of themselves. As one important aspect of the double standard of aging relates to sexuality, we examine research findings concerning women's sexuality in later life. However, we wish to emphasize that our focus on sexuality does *not* imply that we view images of women's aging only in sexual terms. Rather, our point is that stereotypes of older women have focussed on women's purported asexuality, a focus that is imbued with our society's construction of a double standard of aging for women and men.

THE DOUBLE STANDARD OF AGING

Women are viewed as aging sooner and as being less attractive than men at older ages. In her well-known article, Sontag (1972) describes several dimensions of this double standard of aging: women are viewed as sexually ineligible earlier than men; a relationship between an older man and a younger woman is seen as normal while one between an older woman and a younger man is seen as questionable or obscene; and there are two standards of attractiveness for men — the adolescent youth and the distinguised older man — but only one for women — the adolescent, young woman. Cohen (1984, 34) argues that because of the double standard, men see themselves as younger than women their own age: "Many middle-aged husbands have an image of themselves as vital, young, sexual, and virile men married to aging women." The double standard is reflected in elderly people's views of their own attractiveness. In a study of nursing home residents, almost twice as many men as women (31 percent compared to 17 percent) reported that they felt sexually attractive (Wasow and Loeb 1978).

The double standard is partly the result of the general devaluation of women in our society and a tendency to judge women by male standards. More specifically, it may result from the equation of women with biology. If sexuality and youth are equated with reproduction, particularly for women, then the post-menopausal woman becomes "old" often 20 years before a comparably aged man. Post-menopausal women, judged by male standards of continued reproductive function, become viewed as abnormal (a "castrate") and as needing hormone supplements (Wilson and Wilson 1963). Having aged sooner, they continue to be "older" than their male peers: "Our streets abound with them — walking stiffly in twos and threes — seeing little and observing less. It is not unusual to see an erect man of 75 vigorously striding along the golf course, but never a woman of this age" (Wilson and Wilson 1963, 356). Thus de-sexualized by the "sexuality = reproduction" equation, older women become invisible. They are "over the hill" which, as Copper (1985, 48) notes, is "metaphorically out of sight."

This invisibility pertains not only to sexuality but also to power. Copper describes the difficulty older lesbians have participating in lesbian political groups. This problem undoubtedly affects older heterosexual women as well who have formed special political pressure groups such as Displaced Homemakers and the Older Women's League to deal with issues which are important to older women but have not been high on the political agenda of younger women (Cohen 1984).

Another aspect of the definition of older women in terms of their biology is the tendency of younger people to view older women as mothers. Mothers are stereotyped as self-sacrificing, asexual, nurturant, and constraining of their children's freedom. This stereotyping can lead to the following: middle-aged men seeking sexual contact with younger women who remind them less of their mothers than do their middle-aged wives (Cohen 1984); young women projecting their anger towards their own mothers onto other older women (Copper 1985); and therapists having difficulty perceiving the attractiveness of the older women with whom they work (Poggi and Berland 1985).

Consequences of the Double Standard of Aging

The double standard of aging suggests that aging is more difficult for women than it is for men. This view is supported by the information on older women and poverty provided in Chapter 4; the negative images of older women; the finding that women's mental health functioning is lower than men's (Chappell and Havens 1980); and the higher rates of depression for women which are discussed in Chapter 3. However, in large probability sample surveys, women do not usually evaluate their lives as worse than men's lives (Chappell and Havens 1980).

Further, the double standard suggests that middle-aged women are concerned with, and apprehensive about, their appearance. In reality, although middle-aged women are aware of how others perceive them, their appearance is not central to their worries unless aging is incongruous with their needs. Berkun (1983) found that women who are married or securely employed are not concerned with their changing appearance. In fact, many see themselves as more attractive even though they know others do not necessarily share their view. A few women even find that looking older gives them enhanced credibility. On the other hand, some women who are trying to attract men or find work do have negative views about their changed appearance. However, they do not blame themselves and tend to compensate by focussing on family ties and work (Berkun 1983).

Experience with the reality of other women's bodies may also help women see their own bodies less in comparison with society's ideal image. Cohen (1984, 54) quotes a woman who had become involved in exercise who speaks about her experience in the women's locker room: "What you discover when you are surrounded by so many nude women is that the ideal woman who has boyish hips, large firm breasts, flawless skin and long sexy legs, is the rarest thing in the world."

Instead of feeling useless and incompetent when their reproductive capacities cease, many women feel an increased sense of self-esteem and competence during their middle years and into old age (Berkun 1983; Cohen 1984; Giesen and Datan 1980). Cohen (1984) shares the stories of 17 older women who, sometimes in spite of serious physical illness or economic hardship, have achieved goals, changed their lives, and live with dignity. Older women have become political activists in the causes that concern them (Cohen 1984; Kuhn 1984) and serve as an inspiration to younger women in the peace movement (Boucher 1985).

A question readily comes to mind: why is there such a discrepancy between women's objective reality and their subjective one? One possible reason lies in the socialization experience of adult women. It has been suggested that women throughout their adult life face more changes and discontinuities than do men (Kline 1975). They may enter and exit from the labour force several times; they are involved with children who change and demand new responses as they mature; they may relocate to accommodate their husband's work. Learning to cope with these many changes may prepare women to cope with the changes of aging and may make these changes less stressful.

A second reason for women's relatively positive evaluations of their lives may lie in the strength of their support networks, especially the support of other women. A recent Canadian study (MacRae 1986) found that among elderly women, interpersonal relationships form the basis for their self-identities. As we saw in Chapter 6, women rely more on others, both female kin and friends, as confidants and close friends. This may have two effects on their subjective evaluations of their lives. First, women may compare themselves and their lives with those of other women who share their objective situations rather than with men who do not. Second, the emotional support women provide each other may buffer some of the objective hardships, making them seem less important. These support networks may be particularly important for women who have not lived traditional lives, such as single women and lesbians (Atchley *et al.* 1979; Berger 1982; Kimmel 1978).

Another reason that older women may be relatively immune to the potential negative self-image implied by the double standard is that maturity brings a relative freedom from the necessity to conform to society's standards of the ideal woman. Almost all women by old age have not conformed in one way or another to the ideal woman stereotype. In whatever way an individual woman has deviated and coped with the accompanying stigma, she may be better prepared to deal with the stigma of old age. Several authors have suggested that lesbian women may have an easier time dealing with aging for this very reason (*e.g.*, Berger 1982; Kimmel 1978). Divorced, widowed, childless, and single women also know the stigma of non-conformity. Finally, *just being a woman* and, thereby, less valued and less powerful may help women prepare for the experience of old age in an ageist and sexist society.

OLDER WOMEN'S SEXUALITY

From a feminist perspective, sexuality research is rife with the double standard. Men are considered to be more sexual and are studied more frequently in both heterosexual and homosexual populations; sexuality is equated with fertility, making women "asexual" long before men; intercourse is assumed to be synonymous with orgasm; men's problems are attributed to their partners more often than the reverse; and, quantity of sexual activity is studied much more than quality of sexual experience or intimacy (Berger 1982; Kimmel 1978; Laws 1980).

A particularly blatant example of the double standard is Kassel's (1966) recommendation of polygamy for older people. He argues that this practice would solve the problem of too many women for too few men, but it is clear that it is men's problems that would be best solved. For example, Kassel (1966, 217) writes: "... the problem of the frigid wife is eliminated; other partners are available." While the issue of too few men is a problem for many older women, alternatives to marriage such as polygamy are socially unacceptable to most older people, are illegal, and are considered immoral and labelled as deviant (Cavan 1973).

We now turn our attention to a brief review of what we do know of older women's sexuality. This review will be followed by a more detailed examination of what we need to know.

Research Findings

Most of the research conducted in this area is concerned with sexual activity, primarily focussing on coitus, masturbation, and sexual dreams or fantasies. Women who are sexually active in old age are women who were active when they were younger (Christenson and Gagnon 1965; Pfeiffer 1974; Pfeiffer and Davis 1972). Older women report less sexual activity and interest than younger women (Christenson and Gagnon 1965; Christenson and Johnson 1973; George and Weiler 1981; Pfeiffer and Davis 1972; Verwoerdt *et al.* 1969). Men tend to have higher levels of sexual interest and activity, although this difference is much smaller for married than for unmarried people (DeNicola and Peruzza 1974; George and Weiler 1981; Roberts 1980; Verwoerdt *et al.* 1969). Marriage is a much more important determinant of coitus for women than it is for men (Christenson and Gagnon 1965; Christenson and Johnson 1973; Pfeiffer 1974; Pfeiffer and Davis 1972; Verwoerdt *et al.* 1969).

Though single and previously married women report lower levels of coitus than do married women, as many as 30 to 40 percent report engaging in intercourse at age 50 and 8 to 12 percent at age 60. Differences in marital status are less important in the incidence of masturbation and sexual dreams or fantasies (Christenson and Gagnon 1965; Christenson and Johnson 1973).

When a married couple ceases to have intercourse, both the wife and the husband agree that the husband is responsible for stopping (George and Weiler 1981; Pfeiffer *et al.* 1968; Roberts 1980). This may result from the fact that while there is no biological decrease in the orgasmic capacity of older women, older men do experience a slower and less forceful ejaculation (Laws 1980; Pfeiffer 1974). However, capacity for orgasm is never eliminated in men and the male control of cessation of intercourse may have more to do with norms of male initiation of sexuality than with biological differences in responsiveness.

Physical health and institutionalization are two specific factors that influence older women's sexuality. Diabetes can be associated with delayed and inadequate lubrication of the vagina (Weg 1983). Many women with cardiovascular disease fear sexual activity, although there is little reason for any recovered patient to avoid sex (Weg 1983). Probably more detrimental to older women's sexuality is the use and overuse of prescription drugs. Many drugs including tranquillizers, anti-depressants, cardiac drugs, autonomic blockers, anti-hypertensives, and anti-cholinergics can interfere with sexual expression, create sexual performance problems, and/or reduce motivation (Nadelson 1984; Renshaw 1984; Weg 1983).

Institutions are particularly problematic settings for the expression of sexuality. One of the major reasons is lack of privacy, but undoubtedly the patients' relative poor health and accompanying use of drugs, as well as more advanced age, also play a part in decreased sexual activity and interest. The few studies of sexuality in nursing homes indicate very low activity, interest, and feelings of sexual attractiveness. However, interest is generally higher than activity and many individuals express a desire for more information (Kaas 1978; Wasow and Loeb 1978; White 1982).

Areas of Needed Research

Our discussion of what we need to know about older women's sexuality focusses on three areas, all of which emphasize a recognition of the importance of the wider psychological and social context of sexual behaviour. The first area involves *sexual identity*. As with other dimensions of identity, sexual identity is not always, or even usually, identical with behaviour. As women learn about their own sexuality, they form and change their views of themselves as sexual beings. This process is most vividly illustrated by looking at identity formation among lesbian women. There is no single pattern of lesbian identity formation: some women know in childhood and early adolescence that they are attracted to women; others come to this understanding after years of marriage and raising children (Kimmel 1978; Vance and Green 1984). Regardless of the age at which sexual self-identity is established, it is one of major significance and made in the face of strong social disapproval (Kimmel 1978).[1] However, identity as a lesbian does not mean lack of heterosexual experience. Vance and Green (1984) report no difference between early and late identifying lesbians in the number of relationships with men. Kimmel (1978) reports that in one sample 41 percent of lesbians has been married. The reverse is also true. Some heterosexual women have had, or do have, sexual relationships with women (Christenson and Johnson 1973). It is important not to simply assume sexual identity from sexual behaviour. It is also important to study how sexual identity is formed by heterosexual and celibate women, and how sexual and other experiences influence and change one's identity throughout adulthood and old age.

The second area, one in which there is some information but one in which we need to know much more, is how women experience the *quality* of their sexual lives. One way to examine this topic is to ask about intimacy, and the importance of intimacy to sexuality and vice versa. Roberts (1980), in a study of 50 couples who had been married more than 50 years, reports that 20 percent report ongoing intercourse. However, all of the couples, both men and women, report that the physical expression of affection is very important to them. Traupmann (1982) found that among older women with partners, sexual satisfaction is moderately related to satisfaction with the relationship, and that satisfaction with the relationship is higher if the woman reports good physical and psychological health.

Another way to examine the quality of women's sexual experience is to look at the role enjoyment plays in sexual behaviour. Pfeiffer and Davis (1972) found that past enjoyment is more important for women than for men in predicting present sexual interest and frequency of intercourse. Women report that sexuality becomes more satisfying in middle-age (Rubin 1979). Christenson and Johnson (1973) report that married women in their fifties are much more likely to experience orgasm in intercourse if their husbands are the same age rather than younger or older. This latter finding means, perhaps, that equality of power within the relationship enhances women's sexual enjoyment.

Finally, it is most important to study women's sexuality within a broad *social context*. To do this, both a dialectical and a feminist perspective are useful. Sexuality is not an isolated part of life, and is experienced in very different ways by women and men. That men initiate sexual activity more than women, that women are more likely to be victims of sexual violence, that women come to their sexuality later in life, that sexual relationships for married women are often tied to economic dependence, and that older women are often without sexual partners influence women's experience of sexuality.

Another very important part of the context of sexuality is the historical period in which women grow up and grow older. Most studies of sexuality are cross-sectional and very few pay attention to cohort differences (Laws 1980; Traupmann 1984). When cohort differences have been examined, they are clearly present. George and Weiler (1981) found, in a six-year longitudinal study of sexual activity of middle-aged and older people, that cohort differences are as large as age differences for both men and women. Sexual activity declines at the same rate that endorsement of a Victorian sexual code increases in cross-sectional studies of elderly people (Brecher, cited in Traupmann 1984). In a somewhat different vein, a study of college-educated middle-aged mothers and female university students reports that the college students have more liberal attitudes about virginity at marriage and abortion, but less liberal attitudes about non-marriage and childlessness (Yalom *et al.* 1982).

Another important part of the context of sexuality is to study it as an *optional* part of women's lives. Sexual activity is not essential to either physical or psychological well-being. As a motivation, it resembles not so much a drive-reduction or deprivation based model as a social motivation which is feedback-driven, *i.e.*, the less sexual activity, the less motivation and vice versa (Keen 1979; Laws 1980; Thomas 1982).

Sexuality is a part of life and a part of intimacy. However, it is a part that some people choose to live without, and intimacy can and does occur in its absence. The excessive concern some gerontologists have with older peoples' sexuality may reflect less the real needs of elderly persons than a projection of the researcher's fear of aging or loss of potency. We need to view sexuality as a part of some older women's lives and let them tell us of its importance or lack of importance to them. The solution to the problem of too many older women and too few men lies less in the realm of radical sexual alternatives than in the validation of intimacy, which can occur through friendships and confidant relationships.

POLICY IMPLICATIONS

While we have pointed out that many women cope very well with the double standard of aging, this cannot be viewed as a justification for its continuation. It is a social injustice, very much reflective of women's devalued role and status in our society. In terms of its dismantlement, a good starting place is with the media. While the media did not create the double standard, they are important perpetuators of it. Both television and the print media should be monitored, with programmers and advertisers encouraged to include older women in a realistic and positive fashion. We emphasize the term "realistic," for while there is a new trend for women media personalities ("stars") to be older than in past decades, these women (*e.g.*, Jane Fonda, Linda Evans, Joan Collins, Sophia Loren) conform to the stereotypes of female beauty so closely that their "middle-aged stardom" is more representative of a societal denial of aging than an acceptance of the realities of female bodily change with the passage of years. It should be noted that there has been a recent move toward a more realistic portrayal of older women on television, *e.g.*, the *Golden Girls* (although the title leaves much to be desired), and *Murder, She Wrote*.

In the area of sexuality, care facilities should be encouraged to provide a room or rooms that can be used when people desire privacy for sexual and intimacy-related reasons. In addition, given the wide range of medications that can interfere with sexual responsiveness, older women should be informed clearly by their physicians, and also via written information, about the sexual side effects of the drugs, or combination of drugs, that they are taking. Lastly, persons working in face-to-face contact with elderly women should be educated about the diversity of sexual needs among women. In our fight against ageism, we must not fall into the trap of assuming that all older women are highly desirous of sexual relations. Such an assumption can create unnecessary self-doubt and enhance vulnerability.

NOTES

1. Although the gay and lesbian rights movements have provided a strong support organization for lesbian women, the general climate of disapproval still exists. In a national American survey, Snyder and Spreitzer (1976) found that between 54 percent and 92 percent of the sub-groups studied strongly disapproved of homosexuality. In a more recent study of middle-aged mothers and university students, 90 percent of the mothers said they would feel negative or very negative if their daughters established a lesbian relationship, and 78 percent of the students said they would feel negative or very negative if they began a lesbian relationship (Yalom *et al.* 1982).

CHAPTER 8

DIRECTIONS FOR FUTURE RESEARCH

Women's issues are closely tied to both societal (or population) aging and individual aging. With regard to societal aging, women predominate numerically among the elderly population. Women constitute 57 percent of the population aged 65 and over, 65 percent of the population aged 80 and over, and 69 percent of the population aged 90 and over in Canada at the present time.[1] With regard to individual aging, women who survive to age 65 can expect to live more than four years longer than their male counterparts.[2]

In this monograph, we have attempted to provide an overview of what is known about women's aging within the social sciences literature. It is clear that we know quite a bit. As the size of our bibliography testifies, a considerable amount of research has been done, although the portion of this research that is Canadian is quite small.[3] Yet volume alone is no guarantee that we have an accurate and complete portrayal of women's aging. As we have sifted through and synthesized this body of research, we have become aware of a number of problematic features of this literature. These problems fall into three areas: substantive content; theoretical issues; and methodological issues. We now turn to a brief examination of these areas. In so doing, our aim is to suggest directions for future research.

SUBSTANTIVE DIRECTIONS

It is readily apparent that our chapters vary considerably in length. This variability is not due to the fact that we chose to focus on certain topics at the expense of others. Indeed, we wanted to give equal coverage to the issues we felt to be important to the overall area of women and aging. However, we found equal coverage of topics to be an impossible goal because equal coverage does not exist in the research literature.

In general, "family" and "health" are the two areas that researchers have focussed upon in the study of women and aging. Considerably less research has been conducted on issues surrounding women's economic position, occupational careers, sexuality (apart from its health-related aspects, such as menopause), and stereotypes. On one level, the emphasis on family and health issues seems appropriate, given the primacy of women's familial roles and the longer life expectancy of women. On another level, it can be argued that this research concentration reflects male bias and stereotypes about women (*e.g.*, women are wives and mothers who complain about health problems which are mostly "in their heads").

Whatever the reason, the result is a body of literature that fails to take into account the whole spectrum of dimensions of women's lives as they age. We need to know much more about issues relating to women's occupational lives, the quality of their sexual lives, their techniques in managing on limited incomes, their perceptions about needed social and economic change, to name just a few. And, we need to know more about these issues *in relation to* family, health, and other variables.

We are not implying that research relating to health and family should not be continued. There are still many important, unanswered questions relating to these areas. Rather, our point is that other, equally important, topics should be examined in more detail. In addition, research that examines women's lives in totality is needed, including family and health issues but relating them to other aspects of women's lives.

THEORETICAL DIRECTIONS

Too much of the research on women and aging is descriptive, lacking any explicit theoretical basis. Descriptive work is valuable and, indeed, necessary in an area that is under-researched. However, this is not the case with women and aging. We know many facts; we are more than ready for theoretical integration and refinement.

Of the areas discussed in the book, income (and poverty) is one area where the accumulation of facts is impressive but theoretical input is scant. Stereotypes is another area in which description abounds but where theoretical explanations are lacking. We are not making a plea for any particular theoretical perspective, although our leanings toward the interpretive perspective within sociology, the dialectical perspective within psychology, and a feminist perspective in general will be evident to the reader.

An important example of the theoretical impoverishment in the study of women and aging surrounds the fact that there has been very little work concerned with *variations* among women in any of the issues we have discussed. A basic tenet of theory-building and theory-testing is that variations should be examined. For the most part, in this body of research literature the variations that are studied are those comparing women and men. While such comparisons are valuable and should be continued (as long as men are not made the "standard," even implicitly), equally valuable is the study of variations among women in terms of the experience of aging. Indeed, significant theoretical improvement in the area of women and aging can only be accomplished when variations among women are described and explained.

Given the cultural diversity of the Canadian population, we need to conduct research that focusses on ethnic differences in women's aging.[4] We know virtually nothing about the aging experience among native Indian, Chinese, Italian, etc., women. But, this research must be *comparative.* Related to our earlier point, little theoretical contribution will be accomplished by descriptions of, for example, aging Chinese women. Rather, we need to have research that compares Chinese women with other ethnic groups of women on theoretically meaningful dimensions, *e.g.*, the role of kin in support networks; perceptions of bodily change with the passage of time; the inter-relationships between family and work careers; the utilization of western vs. "traditional" forms of health treatments; the experience of grandmothering, childlessness, etc. Other variations that need to be examined more extensively include rural/urban, regional, social class, sexual orientation, and marital status comparisons. A focus on variations, which in our opinion is the largest gap in the existing literature, will not only open the door for theoretical insights and refinements, but will also represent a major step in dismantling the largely implicit assumption that women are a homogeneous group in society who experience aging, both objectively and subjectively, in a similar fashion.

Another area of neglect lies in the failure to incorporate biological variables in the social scientific theories relating to women and aging (Rossi 1980). Aging clearly has a physiological dimension, and one that may differ for women and men in any number of ways, *e.g.*, endocrine changes. We need to incorporate this dimension into our theorizing about women's aging and sex differences in aging.

As feminists, we are skeptical of these variables for ideological reasons; as social scientists, we recognize the importance of examining physiological and biological factors, in interaction with social and psychological ones, for a fuller understanding of women's aging. It is the study of biological variables in isolation that is problematic on both ideological and scientific grounds. Biological variables studied and interpreted in a psychological, economic, sociological and historical context lead to accurate science and a more complex world view. Feminists need to be interested and involved in this work.

METHODOLOGICAL REDIRECTION

Social science research contains a methodological bias in favour of quantitative rigour. Counting and statistical analysis are considered "better science" than qualitative accounts and techniques focussing upon subjective dimensions of life. It is our opinion that both types of approaches have their place. The subject matter should dictate the approach used, rather than a blind adherence to quantitative methodologies.

Women's roles and status in society have operated to reinforce and enhance the subjective and qualitative dimensions of their lives. To the degree that this is true, more qualitative methodological approaches need to be incorporated into the study of women and aging. As we saw in Chapter 6, the quality of interpersonal contact is much more closely associated with older women's sense of well-being and satisfaction with life than is the quantity of contacts. A recent Canadian study (Wister and Strain 1986) provides compelling evidence that the generally accepted proposition that widowers face a more difficult adjustment to widowhood than widows is erroneous in that it fails to consider differences between women and men in the subjective or qualitative evaluations of their situation and in their psycho-social needs as mediated by prior gender role socialization.

It is crucial that future research obtain women's (and men's) subjective evaluations and definitions of the phenomena studied. The importance of this is strikingly illustrated in the research of Harkins (1978), as discussed in Chapter 6. It will be recalled that only 1.3 percent of Harkins's sample agreed with the conventionally used, by social scientists, definition of the empty nest. Such a finding challenges seriously all of the research on the empty nest that uses the researcher's definition only. More importantly, it raises questions about *all* research that uses (imposes?) an "objective" definition of a phenomenon or event, a query that is particularly applicable to quantitative research. If we are that far off base in terms of definition of the empty nest, in what other areas are our operationalization of concepts meaningless to the people who are studied, thereby producing meaningless results?

In terms of research design, more longitudinal studies are needed. While this plea is a common one, we recognize that the realities of research funding and pressures on academics for quick results preclude a major change away from the predominance of cross-sectional designs.

If we are going to have to rely on cross-sectional studies, we can, however, improve their sophistication in both execution and interpretation. In terms of execution, cross-sectional studies can be improved greatly by controlling for theoretically relevant variables. For example, in the area of women's sexual expression in later life, studies should control for factors such as health status, drugs taken, age, opportunity, interest, and past experience and/or practices. No study to date has controlled simultaneously for all these variables (Laws 1980).

In terms of interpretation, we must be careful not to make generalizations from the findings of one age group or cohort. As Rossi (1980) points out, virtually everything we know about the so-called mid-life crisis has been obtained from a particular cohort of women and men — persons born in the 1930s for the most part. This cohort is atypical in many ways: it is numerically small; it reached young adulthood in the prosperous years following World War II when jobs and promotions were readily available; it married young and had children young. Its experience at mid-life may be more a reflection of its unique place in history and its social and economic context than anything instrinsic to mid-life *per se*. A sensitivity to the possibility of such "cohort particularity" will enhance greatly our interpretations of research findings regarding adult development and aging.

Our last suggestion for methodological improvement concerns the reporting of research findings. We found numerous studies where large proportional or random samples were studied and patterns of relationships were reported (*e.g.*, between contact with children and well-being) *but* where no information was provided as to whether the patterns differed for women and men. In most cases, the samples were large enough so that such analysis could be performed. We suspect that the researchers tested, found no difference between women and men, and then combined the data, but we do not know for sure. If there are no gender differences, then it makes sense to report a single pattern of results, *but only* after informing the reader that no differences were found. One example of this lack of attention to gender differences occurs in a study by Cicirelli (1983) which examines the intentions of adult males and females to help elderly mothers, but provides no analysis of gender differences. Given that we know that women are much more likely than men to provide help to their mothers, it is important to know whether there are gender differences in intentions to provide help.

As we mentioned, we suspect that this failure to provide sex or gender differences in published studies stems from the fact that the researchers did not find a difference. This suspicion is based upon our knowledge of a scientific norm that holds that a finding of no difference is not considered to be an important finding. However, in our opinion, this norm is highly questionable: a finding of no difference can be as important, perhaps even more important in some cases, as a finding of significant difference.

Two results emanate from this tendency not to report findings for both women and men. One, we cannot be sure what differences do exist between women and men. Two, if we are correct in our assumption that findings of no difference are under-reported, then the research literature presents an overall picture that exaggerates differences between women and men in terms of adult development and aging.

SOME CONCLUDING COMMENTS

While writing this monograph, we were struck time and time again by findings that indicated the degree to which women cope well with aging. Despite an overall social and economic environment that devalues women in general and older women in particular, women are not "broken down." Women compensate for their relative social, economic, and political powerlessness through the construction of rich interpersonal ties, both within the family (particularly the mother-daughter relationship) and through close, intimate friendships with other women. They also gain self-esteem through coping with and resisting the social institutions which devalue them.

In part, then, "public" anonymity, invisibility, and vulnerability are counteracted by "private" satisfactions and achievements. While women have worked out this strategy for individual well-being, it is a strategy constructed in response to an alienating social structure that excludes women from full and equal participation in the wider society.

With industrialization, and its attendant separation of the home and the workplace, came the social dichotomy of the private (women's) domain and the public (men's) domain. We have seen throughout this monograph that few inroads have been made in post-industrial society to dismantle this artificial, gender-specific distinction. It is our hope that research and research-based policy changes will provide the stimuli that will provide women (and men) with opportunities to be actively involved in both domains. Then women will not need to resort to "survival" tactics or strategies to deal with the aging experience. This is not to say that women will, or should, dispense with their rich interpersonal ties. Rather, our point is that structural change that creates social and economic equality between women and men will produce a situation in which individual women will be able to maximize their life-choices as they age.

NOTES

1. These figures are calculated from data presented in Table 2.1.
2. This datum is taken from Figure 2.1.
3. Canadian-based research articles and reports, including government publications, total 66 in our bibliography. In constrast, there are 237 references to other (largely American) sources. Both figures exclude general references to the social science literature on aging and to research cited that is only indirectly related to our topic.
4. However, the various definitional problems in assessing "ethnicity" must be addressed (Rosenthal 1986a). For an overview of ethnicity and aging, see Driedger and Chappell (1987).

BIBLIOGRAPHY

Adams, G. M., and H. A. deVries
1973 "Physiological Effects of Exercise Training Regimen Upon Women Aged 52 to 79." *Journal of Gerontology* 28:50–55.

Ahammer, I. M.
1973 "Social-learning Theory as a Framework for the Study of Adult Personality Development." In P. B. Baltes and K. W. Schaie (eds.), *Life-Span Developmental Psychology: Personality and Socialization*. New York: Academic Press.

Aitken, J. M., D. M. Hart, and R. Lindsay
1973 "Estrogen Replacement Therapy for Prevention of Osteoporosis after Oophorectomy." *British Medical Journal* 3:515–18.

Aldous, J., E. Klaus, and D. M. Klein
1985 "The Understanding Heart: Aging Parents and Their Favorite Children." *Child Development* 56:303–16.

Anderson, M.
1971 *Family Structure in 19th Century Lancashire*. Cambridge: Cambridge University Press.

Arensen, S. J.
1978 "Age and Sex Preferences in the Probability Preferences of Children." *Psychological Reports* 43:697–98.

Arling, G.
1976 "The Elderly Widow and Her Family, Neighbors, and Friends." *Journal of Marriage and the Family* 38:757–68.

Armstrong, P.
1984 *Labour Pains: Women's Work in Crisis*. Toronto: The Women's Press.

Atchley, R. C.
1976a "Orientation Toward the Job and Retirement Adjustment Among Women." In J. F. Gubrium (ed.), *Time, Roles, and Self in Old Age*. New York: Behavioral Publications.

1976b "Selected Social and Psychological Differences Between Men and Women in Later Life." *Journal of Gerontology* 31:204–11.

1982 "The Process of Retirement: Comparing Women and Men." In M. Szinovacz (ed.), *Women's Retirement: Policy Implications of Recent Research*. Beverly Hills, Calif.: Sage.

Atchley, R. C., and S. L. Corbett
1977 "Older Women and Jobs." In L. E. Troll, J. Israel, and K. Israel (eds.), *Looking Ahead: A Woman's Guide to the Problems and Joys of Growing Older*. Englewood Cliffs, N.J.: Prentice-Hall.

Atchley, R. C., L. Pignatiello, and E. Shaw
1979 "Interactions with Family and Friends: Marital Status and Occupational Differences among Older Women." *Research on Aging* 1:83–96.

Babchuck, N.
   1978–79 "Aging and Primary Relations." *International Journal of Aging and Human Development* 9:137–51.
Bachrach, C. A.
   1980   "Childlessness and Social Isolation." *Journal of Marriage and the Family* 42:627–36.
Back, K.
   1974   "The Three-generation Household in Pre-industrial Society: Norm or Expedient." Paper presented at the annual meeting of the Gerontological Society, Portland, Oregon.
Baker, M.
   1984   "His and Her Divorce Research: New Theoretical Directions in Canadian and American Research." *Journal of Comparative Family Studies* 15:17–28.
Ballau, R. L., and R. M. Buchan
   1978   "Study Shows that Gender is Not a Major Factor in Accident Etiology." *Occupational Health and Safety* 47:54–58.
Bankoff, E. A.
   1983   "Social Support and Adaptation to Widowhood." *Journal of Marriage and the Family* 45:827–39.
Barer, M. L., R. G. Evans, C. Hertzman, and J. Lomas
   1986   "Toward Efficient Aging: Rhetoric and Evidence." Paper presented at the Third Canadian Conference on Health Economics, Winnipeg, May.
Barnett, R. C., and G. K. Baruch
   1978   "Women in the Middle Years: A Critique of Research and Theory." *Psychology of Women Quarterly* 3:187–97.
Barrett, C. J.
   1977   "Women in Widowhood." *Signs* 2:856–68.
   1978   "Effectiveness of Widows' Groups in Facilitating Change." *Journal of Consulting and Clinical Psychology* 46:120–31.
   1981   "Intimacy in Widowhood." *Psychology of Women Quarterly* 5:473–87.
Bart, P. B.
   1971   "Depression in Middle-aged Women." In V. Gornick and B. K. Moran (eds.), *Women in Sexist Society*. New York: Signet.
Baruch, G., and R. C. Barnett
   1983   "Adult Daughters' Relationships with their Mothers." *Journal of Marriage and the Family* 45:601–606.
Baruch, G., R. Barnett, and C. Rivers
   1983   *Life Prints: New Patterns of Work and Love for Today's Woman.* New York: New American Library.
Beckman, L. J., and B. B. Houser
   1982   "The Consequences of Childlessness on the Social-psychological Well-being of Older Women." *Journal of Gerontology* 37:243–50.
Bem, S. L.
   1974   "The Measurement of Psychological Androgyny." *Journal of Consulting and Clinical Psychology* 42:155–62.

Berger, R.
1982   "The Unseen Minority: Older Gays and Lesbians." *Social Work* 27:236–42.

Berkun, C. S.
1983   "Changing Appearance for Women in the Middle Years of Life: Trauma?" In E. W. Markson (ed.), *Older Women: Issues and Prospects.* Lexington, Mass.: Lexington Books.

Bernstein, B., and R. Kane
1981   "Physicians' Attitudes Toward Female Patients." *Medical Care* 19:600–607.

Bielby, D. D. V., and W. T. Bielby
1984   "Work Commitment, Sex-role Attitudes, and Women's Employment." *American Sociological Review* 49:234–47.

Binstock, R. H.
1983   "The Aged as Scapegoat." *The Gerontologist* 23:136–43.

Binstock, R. H., and E. Shanas (eds.)
1985   *Handbook of Aging and the Social Sciences* (2nd ed.). New York: Van Nostrand Reinhold.

Birnbaum, J. A.
1975   "Life Patterns and Self-esteem in Gifted Family-oriented and Career-committed Women." In M. T. S. Mednick, S. S. Tangri, and L. W. Hoffman (eds.), *Women and Achievement: Social and Motivational Analyses.* New York: Wiley.

Black, S. M., and C. E. Hill
1984   "The Psychological Well-being of Women in Their Middle Years." *Psychology of Women Quarterly* 8:282–91.

Block, M. R.
1982   "Professional Women: Work Pattern as a Correlate of Retirement Satisfaction." In M. Szinovacz (ed.), *Women's Retirement: Policy Implications of Recent Research.* Beverly Hills, Calif.: Sage.

Bond, J. B., Jr.
1982   "Volunteerism and Life Satisfaction Among Older Adults." *Canadian Counsellor* 16:168–72.

Borland, D. C.
1982   "A Cohort Analysis Approach to the Empty Nest Syndrome among Three Ethnic Groups of Women: A Theoretical Position." *Journal of Marriage and the Family* 44:117–29.

Boston Women's Health Book Collective
1984   *The New Our Bodies, Our Selves.* New York: Simon and Schuster.

Boucher, S.
1985   "Half a Map." *Sinister Wisdom* 28:104–109.

Brody, E. M.
1981   "Women in the Middle and Family Help to Older People." *The Gerontologist* 21:471–80.

Brody, E. M., P. T. Johnson, and M. C. Fulcomer
1984   "What Should Adult Children Do for Elderly Parents? Opinions and Preferences of Three Generations of Women." *Journal of Gerontology* 39:736–46.

Brody, E. M., and C. B. Schoonover
   1986   "Patterns of Parent-Care When Adult Daughters Work and When They
           Do Not." *The Gerontologist* 26:372–81.
Burch, T. K.
   1985   *Family History Survey: Preliminary Findings*. Ottawa: Statistics
           Canada Catalogue No. 99-955.
Burgess, E. (ed.)
   1960   *Aging in Western Societies*. Chicago: University of Chicago Press.
Burwell, E. J.
   1984   "Sexism in Social Science Research on Aging." In J. M. Vickers (ed.),
           Taking Sex into Account: The Policy Consequences of Sexist Research.
           Ottawa: Carleton University Press.
Carlson, W. L.
   1972   "Alcohol Usage of the Nighttime Driver." *Journal of Safety Research*
           4:12–25.
Cavan, R. S.
   1973   "Speculations on Innovations to Conventional Marriages in Old Age."
           The Gerontologist 13:409–11.
Chambre, S. M.
   1984   "Is Volunteering a Substitute for Role Loss in Old Age? An Empirical
           Test of Activity Theory." *The Gerontologist* 24:292–98.
Chappell, N.
   1983   "Informal Support Networks Among the Elderly." *Research on Aging*
           5:77–99.
Chappell, N. L., and B. Havens
   1980   "Old and Female: Testing the Double Jeopardy Hypothesis." *The Socio-
           logical Quarterly* 21:157–71.
Chappell, N. L., L. A. Strain, and A. A. Blandford
   1986   *Aging and Health Care: A Social Perspective*. Toronto: Holt, Rinehart
           and Winston.
Cherpas, C. C.
   1985   "Dual-career Families: Terminology, Typologies, and Work and Family
           Issues." *Journal of Counseling and Development* 63:616–20.
Chiriboga, D. A.
   1981   "Adaptation to Marital Separation in Later and Earlier Life." *Journal of
           Gerontology* 37:109–14.
Christenson, C. V., and J. H. Gagnon
   1965   "Sexual Behavior in a Group of Older Women." *Journal of Gerontology*
           20:351–56.
Christenson, C. V., and A. B. Johnson
   1973   "Sexual Patterns in a Group of Older Never-married Women." *Journal
           of Geriatric Psychiatry* 6:80–98.
Christiansen, C., M. S. Christensen, P. McNair, C. Hagen, K. Stocklund, and
           I. Transbol
   1980   "Prevention of Early Postmenopausal Bone Loss: Controlled 2-year
           Study of 315 Normal Females." *European Journal of Clinical Investiga-
           tion* 10:273–79.

Cicirelli, V. G.
   1983   "Adult Children's Attachment and Helping Behavior to Elderly Parents: A Path Model." *Journal of Marriage and the Family* 45:815–25.
Cleary, P. D., D. Mechanic, and J. R. Greenley
   1982   "Sex Differences in Medical Care Utilization: An Empirical Investigation." *Journal of Health and Social Behavior* 23:106–19.
Cleveland, W. P., and D. T. Gianturco
   1976   "Remarriage Probability after Widowhood: A Retrospective Method." *Journal of Gerontology* 31:99–103.
Coet, L. J., and P. J. McDermott
   1979   "Sex, Instructional Set, and Group Make-up: Organismic and Situational Factors Influencing Risk-taking." *Psychological Reports* 44:1283–94.
Cohen, L.
   1984   *Small Expectations: Society's Betrayal of Older Women*. Toronto: McClelland and Stewart.
Coleman, L. M., and T. C. Antonucci
   1983   "Impact of Work on Women at Midlife." *Developmental Psychology* 19:290–94.
Comfort, A.
   1979   *The Biology of Senescence* (3rd ed.). Edinburgh: Churchill Livingstone.
Connelly, P.
   1978   *Last Hired First Fired: Women and the Canadian Work Force*. Toronto: The Women's Press.
Connidis, I.
   1982   "Women and Retirement: The Effect of Multiple Careers on Retirement Adjustment." *Canadian Journal on Aging* 1:17–27.
   1985   "The Service Needs of Older People: Implications for Public Policy." *Canadian Journal on Aging* 4:3–10.
Connidis, I., and J. Rempel
   1983   "The Living Arrangements of Older Residents: The Role of Gender, Marital Status, Age, and Family Size." *Canadian Journal on Aging* 2:91–105.
Cooperstock, R.
   1978   "Sex Differences in Psychotropic Drug Use." *Social Science and Medicine* 12B:179–86.
Copper, B.
   1985   "The View from Over the Hill: Notes on Ageism Between Lesbians." *Trivia* 7:48–63.
Cowgill, D.
   1974   "The Aging of Populations and Societies." *The Annals* 415:1018.
Creecy, R. F., W. E. Berg, and R. Wright, Jr.
   1985   "Loneliness Among the Elderly: A Causal Approach." *Journal of Gerontology* 40:487–93.
Crossman, L., C. London, and C. Barry
   1981   "Older Women Caring for Disabled Spouses: A Model for Supportive Services." *The Gerontologist* 21:464–70.

Cumming, E., and W. Henry
1961 *Growing Old: The Process of Disengagement*. New York: Basic Books.

Curran, V., and S. Golombok
1985 *Bottling It Up*. London: Faber and Faber.

Daniell, H. W.
1976 "Osteoporosis of the Slender Smoker: Vertebral Compression Fractures and Loss of Metacarpal Cortex in Relation to Postmenopausal Cigarette Smoking and Lack of Obesity." *Archives of Internal Medicine* 136:298–304.

Davis, K., and P. van den Oever
1981 "Age Relations and Public Policy in Industrial Society." *Population and Development Review* 7:1–19.

Davis, M. A.
1981 "Sex Differences in Reporting Osteoarthritic Symptoms: A Sociomedical Approach." *Journal of Health and Social Behavior* 22:298–310.

Demos, J.
1968 "Families in Colonial Bristol, Rhode Island: An Exercise in Historical Demography." *William and Mary Quarterly* (3rd Series) 22:264–86.

DeNicola, P., and M. Peruzza
1974 "Sex and the Aged." *Journal of the American Geriatrics Society* 22:380–83.

Depner, C. E., and B. Ingersoll
1982 "Employment Status and Social Support: The Experience of the Mature Woman." In M. Szinovacz (ed.), *Women's Retirement: Policy Implications of Recent Research*. Beverly Hills, Calif.: Sage.

Depner, C. E., and B. Ingersoll-Dayton
1985 "Conjugal Social Support: Patterns in Later Life." *Journal of Gerontology* 40:761–66.

Doherty, W. J., and C. Baldwin
1985 "Shifts and Stability in Locus of Control During the 1970s: Divergence of the Sexes." *Journal of Personality and Social Psychology* 48:1048–53.

Dowd, J. J.
1980 *Stratification Among the Aged*. Monterey, Calif.: Brooks/Cole.

Dreidger, L., and N. L. Chappell
1987 *Aging and Ethnicity: Toward an Interface*. Toronto: Butterworths.

Dupont, W. D., and D. L. Page
1985 "Risk Factors for Breast Cancer in Women with Proliferative Breast Disease." *New England Journal of Medicine* 312:146–51.

Elder, G. H., Jr.
1978 "Approaches to Social Change and the Family." *American Journal of Sociology* 84:S1–S38.

Enterline, P. E.
1961 "Causes of Death Responsible for Recent Increases in Sex Mortality Differentials in the United States." *Milbank Memorial Fund Quarterly* 39:312–28.

Erikson, E.
1980a *Identity and the Life Cycle* (Re-issue). New York: Norton.

1980b "On the Generational Cycle: An Address." *International Journal of Psycho-Analysis* 61:213–23.

1982 *The Life Cycle Completed.* New York: Norton.

Fenwick, R., and C. M. Burresi

1981 "Health Consequences of Marital Status and Change Among the Elderly: A Comparison of Cross-sectional and Longitudinal Analysis." *Journal of Health and Social Behavior* 22:106–16.

Ferree, M. M.

1984 "Class, Housework, and Happiness: Women's Work and Life Satisfaction." *Sex Roles* 11:1057–74.

Ferrence, R.

1980 "Sex Differences in the Prevalence of Problem Drinking." *Research Advances in Alcohol and Drug Problems* 5:69–124.

Finlayson, J.

1982 "The Sexual Politics of Sickness." *Homemaker's Magazine* 17(5):24–38.

Fisher, L. R.

1983 "Transition into Grandmotherhood." *International Journal of Aging and Human Development* 16:67–77.

Fox, J. H.

1977 "Effects of Retirement and Former Work Life on Women's Adaptation in Old Age." *Journal of Gerontology* 32:196–202.

Gee, E. M.

1986 "The Life Course of Canadian Women: An Historical and Demographic Analysis." *Social Indicators Research* 18:263–83.

Gee, E. M., and J. E. Veevers

1983 "Accelerating Sex Differentials in Mortality: An Analysis of Contributing Factors." *Social Biology* 30:75–85.

George, L., and S. Weiler

1981 "Sexuality in Middle and Later Life: The Effects of Age, Cohort and Gender." *Archives of General Psychiatry* 38:919–23.

George, L. K., G. G. Fillerbaum, and E. Palmore

1984 "Sex Differences in Antecedents and Consequences of Retirement." *Journal of Gerontology* 39:364–71.

Giesen, C. B., and N. Datan

1980 "The Competent Older Woman." In C. B. Giesen and N. Datan (eds.), *Transitions in Aging.* New York: Academic Press.

Gigy, L. L.

1985–86 "Preretired and Retired Women's Attitudes Towards Retirement." *International Journal of Aging and Human Development* 22:31–44.

Gilford, R.

1984 "Contrasts in Marital Satisfaction Throughout Old Age: An Exchange Theory Analysis." *Journal of Gerontology* 39:325–33.

Gilligan, C.

1982 *In a Different Voice: Psychological Theory and Women's Development.* Cambridge, Mass.: Harvard University Press.

Glenn, N. D., and S. McLanahan

1981 "The Effects of Offspring on the Psychological Well-being of Older Adults." *Journal of Marriage and the Family* 43:409–21.

1982   "Children and Marital Happiness: A Further Specification of the Relationship." *Journal of Marriage and the Family* 44:63–72.

Gove, W.
1984   "Gender Differences in Mental and Physical Illness: The Effects of Fixed Roles and Nurturant Roles." *Social Science and Medicine* 19:77–91.

Gove, W., and M. Hughes
1979   "Possible Causes of the Apparent Sex Differences in Physical Health: An Empirical Investigation." *American Sociological Review* 44:126–46.

Graney, M. J.
1979   "An Exploration of Social Factors Influencing the Sex Differential in Mortality." *Sociological Symposium* 28:1–26.

Gratton, B., and M. R. Haug
1983   "Decision and Adaptation: Research on Female Retirement." *Research on Aging* 5:59–75.

Gubrium, J. F.
1974   "Marital Desolation and the Evaluation of Everyday Life in Old Age." *Journal of Marriage and the Family* 36:107–13.

Harkins, E. B.
1978   "Effects of Empty Nest Transition on Self-Report of Psychological and Physical Well-being." *Journal of Marriage and the Family* 40:549–56.

Harrison, J.
1978   "Warning: The Male Sex Role May be Dangerous to Your Health." *Journal of Social Issues* 34:65–96.

Haynes, S., and M. Feinleib
1980   "Women, Work and Coronary Heart Disease: Prospective Findings from the Framingham Heart Study." *American Journal of Public Health* 70:133–41.

Health and Welfare Canada
1982a   *Better Pensions for Canadians.* Ottawa: Minister of Supply and Services.
1982b   *Better Pensions for Canadians: Focus on Women.* Ottawa: Minister of Supply and Services.
1982c   *Canadian Governmental Report on Aging.* Ottawa: Minister of Supply and Services.

Heligman, L.
1983   "Patterns of Sex Differentials in Mortality in Less Developed Countries." In A. D. Lopez and L. T. Ruzicka (eds.), *Sex Differentials in Mortality: Trends, Determinants and Consequences.* Canberra: Australian National University Press.

Henderson, C., and G. P. Canellos
1980   "Cancer of the Breast — the Past Decade. Part I." *New England Journal of Medicine* 302:17–30.

Hendricks, J. A.
1977   "Women and Leisure." In L. E. Troll, J. Israel, and K. Israel (eds.), *Looking Ahead: A Woman's Guide to the Problems and Joys of Growing Older.* Englewood Cliffs, N.J.: Prentice-Hall.

Herzog, J.
1986   Personal communication.

Hess, B. B.
1985　"Aging Policies and Old Women: The Hidden Agenda." In A. S. Rossi (ed.), *Gender and the Life Course*. New York: Aldine.

Hibbard, J. H., and C. R. Pope
1983　"Gender Roles, Illness Orientation and Use of Medical Services." *Social Science and Medicine* 17:129–37.

Hicks, R., H. H. Funkenstein, M. W. Dysken, and J. M. Davis
1980　"Geriatric Psychopharmacology." In J. E. Birren and R. B. Sloane (eds.), *Handbook of Mental Health and Aging*. Englewood Cliffs, N.J.: Prentice-Hall.

Himmelfarb, S.
1984　"Age and Sex Differences in the Mental Health of Older Persons." *Journal of Consulting and Clinical Psychology* 52:844–56.

Hooker, K., and D. G. Ventis
1984　"Work Ethic, Daily Activities and Retirement Satisfaction." *Journal of Gerontology* 39:478–84.

Hornstein, G. A., and S. Wapner
1985　"Modes of Experiencing and Adapting to Retirement." *International Journal of Aging and Human Development* 21:291–315.

Horowitz, A.
1985　"Sons and Daughters as Caregivers to Older Parents: Differences in Role Performance and Consequences." *The Gerontologist* 25:612–17.

Houser, B. B., S. L. Berkman, and L. J. Beckman
1984　"The Relative Rewards and Costs of Childlessness for Older Women." *Psychology of Women Quarterly* 8:395–98.

Hutter, R. V. P.
1985　"Goodbye to Fibrocystic Disease." *New England Journal of Medicine* 312:179–81.

Jacobson, C. J.
1974　"Rejection of the Retiree Role: A Study of Female Industrial Workers in Their 50s." *Human Relations* 29:477–92.

Jarrett, W. H.
1985　"Caregiving within Kinship Systems: Is Affection Really Necessary?" *The Gerontologist* 25:5–10.

Jewson, R. H.
1982　"After Retirement: An Exploratory Study of the Professional Woman." In M. Szinovacz (ed.), *Women's Retirement: Policy Implications of Recent Research*. Beverly Hills, Calif.: Sage.

Johnson, C. L., and D. J. Catalano
1981　"Childless Elderly and Their Family Supports." *The Gerontologist* 21:610–18.

Jourard, S. M.
1974　"Some Lethal Aspects of the Male Sex Role." In J. H. Pleck and J. Sawyer (eds.), *Men and Masculinity*. Englewood Cliffs, N.J.: Prentice-Hall.

Kaas, J.
1978　"Sexual Expression of the Elderly in Nursing Homes." *The Gerontologist* 18:372–78.

Kahana, E., and B. Kahana
    1971   "Theoretical and Research Perspectives on Grandparenthood." *Aging and Human Development* 2:261–68.
Kaplan, F. S.
    1985   "Osteoporosis." In S. Golub and R. J. Freedman (eds.), *Health Needs of Women as They Age*. New York: Haworth Press.
Kass, N.
    1964   "Risk in Decision Making as a Function of Age, Sex and Probability Preference." *Child Development* 35:577–82.
Kassel, V.
    1966   "Polygamy After 60." *Geriatrics* 21:214–18.
Kaye, L. W., and A. Monk
    1984   "Sex Role Traditions and Retirement from Academe." *The Gerontologist* 24:420–26.
Keating, N., and B. Jeffrey
    1983   "Work Careers of Ever Married and Never Married Retired Women." *The Gerontologist* 23:416–21.
Keen, S.
    1979   "Some Ludicrous Theses about Sexuality." *Journal of Humanistic Psychology* 19:15–22.
Keith, P. M.
    1982   "Working Women Versus Homemakers: Retirement Resources and Correlates of Well-being." In M. Szinovacz (ed.), *Women's Retirement: Policy Implications of Recent Research*. Beverly Hills, Calif.: Sage.
Kilty, K. M., and J. H. Behling
    1985   "Predicting the Retirement Intentions and Attitudes of Professional Workers." *Journal of Gerontology* 40:219–27.
Kimball, M. M.
    1979   "Returning to Work or School: Women's Career Decisions." *Atlantis* 4:212–21.
Kimmel, D. C.
    1978   "Adult Development and Aging: A Gay Perspective." *Journal of Social Issues* 34:113–30.
Kline, C.
    1975   "The Socialization Process of Women." *The Gerontologist* 15:486–92.
Kovar, M. G.
    1977   "Health of the Elderly and Use of Health Services." *Public Health Reports* 92:9–19.
Kroeger, N.
    1982   "Preretirement Preparation: Sex Differences in Access, Sources, and Use." In M. Szinovacz (ed.), *Women's Retirement: Policy Implications of Recent Research*. Beverly Hills, Calif.: Sage.
Krotki, K., D. Odynak, T. R. Balakrishnan, and E. Lapierre-Adamcyk
    1986   "First Time Worker, First Time Wife, First Time Mother." Paper presented at the annual meeting of the Canadian Population Society, Winnipeg, June.

Kuhn, M.
    1974   "Grass-roots Gray Power." *Prime Time* 2:4–6.
Labour Canada
    1983   *Part-time Work in Canada: Report of the Commission of Inquiry into Part-time Work.* Ottawa: Minister of Supply and Services.
    1986   *Women in the Labour Force: 1985–1986 Edition.* Ottawa: Minister of Supply and Services.
Lang, A. M., and E. M. Brody
    1983   "Characteristics of Middle Aged Daughters and Help to Their Elderly Mothers." *Journal of Marriage and Family* 45:193–202.
Larson, R., J. Zuzanek, and R. Mannell
    1985   "Being Alone Versus Being with People: Disengagement in the Daily Experience of Older Adults." *Journal of Gerontology* 40:375–81.
Laslett, P.
    1983   *The World We Have Lost* (3rd. ed.). New York: Scribner.
    1985   "Societal Development and Aging." in R. H. Binstock and E. Shanas (eds.), *Handbook of Aging and the Social Sciences* (2nd ed.). New York: Van Nostrand Reinhold.
Laslett, P., and R. Wall (eds.)
    1972   *Household and Family in Past Time.* Cambridge: Cambridge University Press.
Laurence, M. W.
    1961   "Sources of Satisfaction in the Lives of Working Women." *Journal of Gerontology* 16:163–67.
Laws, J. L.
    1980   "Female Sexuality Through the Life-span." In P. Baltes and O. Brim, Jr. (eds.), *Life-Span Development and Behavior (Vol. 3).* New York: Academic Press.
Lee, G. R., and E. Ellithorpe
    1982   "Intergenerational Exhange and Subjective Well-being Among the Elderly." *Journal of Marriage and the Family* 4:217–24.
Lever, J.
    1976   "Sex Differences in the Games Children Play." *Social Problems* 23:479–87.
Lewis, S. G.
    1979   *Sunday's Women: Lesbian Lifestyles.* Boston, Mass.: Beacon Press.
Liang, R., L. Dvorkin, E. Kahana, and F. Mazian
    1980   "Social Interaction and Morale: A Re-examination." *Journal of Gerontology* 35:746–57.
Lichtenstein, G.
    1981   *Machisma: Women and Daring.* Garden City: Doubleday.
Lindsay, R., J. M. Aitken, J. B. Anderson, D. M. Hart, E. B. MacDonald, and A. C. Clark
    1976   "Long-term Prevention of Postmenopausal Osteoporosis by Oestrogen." *Lancet* 1:1038–40.
Lindsay, R., A. MacLean, A. Kraszewski, D. M. Hart, A. C. Clark, and J. Garwood
    1978   "Bone Response to Termination of Oestrogen Treatment." *Lancet* 1:1325–27.

Livson, F. B.
   1981   "Paths to Psychological Health in the Middle Years: Sex Differences." In D. H. Eichorn, J. A. Clausen, N. Maan, M. P. Hoznik and P. H. Mussen (eds.), *Present and Past in Middle Life*. New York: Academic Press.

Longino, C. F., Jr., and A. Lipman
   1981   "Married and Spouseless Men and Women in Planned Retirement Communities: Support Network Differentials." *Journal of Marriage and the Family* 43:169–77.

Lopez, A. D., and L. T. Ruzicka
   1983   "Introduction." In A. D. Lopez and L. T. Ruzicka (eds.), *Sex Differentials in Mortality: Trends, Determinants and Consequences*. Canberra: Australian National University Press.

Lorde, A.
   1980   *The Cancer Journals*. San Francisco, Calif.: Spinsters Ink.

Love, S. M., R. S. Gelman, and W. Silen
   1982   "Fibrocystic 'Disease' of the Breast: A Non-disease?" *New England Journal of Medicine* 307:1010–14.

Lovell-Troy, L. A.
   1983   "Anomia among Employed Wives and Housewives: An Exploratory Analysis." *Journal of Marriage and the Family* 45:301–10.

Lowenthal, M. F., and C. Haven
   1968   "Interaction and Adaptation: Intimacy as a Critical Variable." *American Sociological Review* 33:20–30.

Lowenthal, M. F., and C. Haven
   1968   "Interaction and Adaptation: Intimacy as a Critical Variable." *American Sociological Review* 33:20–30.

Luxton, M.
   1981   "Taking on the Double Day: Housewives as a Reserve Army of Labour." *Atlantis* 7:12–22.

Mack, T. M., M. C. Pike, B. E. Henderson, R. I. Pfeffer, V. R. Gerkins, M. Arthur, and S. E. Brown
   1976   "Estrogens and Endometrial Cancer in a Retirement Community." *New England Journal of Medicine* 294:1262–67.

Mackie, M.
   1986   "Gender Relations." In R. Hagedorn (ed.), *Sociology* (3rd ed.). Toronto: Holt, Rinehart and Winston.

McCranie, E. W., A. J. Horowitz, and R. M. Martin
   1978   "Alleged Sex-role Stereotyping in the Assessment of Women's Physical Complaints: A Study of General Practitioners." *Social Science and Medicine* 12:111–16.

McDaniel, S. A.
   1986   *Canada's Aging Population*. Toronto: Butterworths.

McKain, W. C.
   1972   "A New Look at Older Marriages." *The Family Coordinator* 21:61–69.

McKim, W. A., and B. L. Mishara
   1987   *Drugs and Aging*. Toronto: Butterworths.

McKinlay, S. M., and M. Jeffreys
   1974   "The Menopausal Syndrome." *British Journal of Preventive and Social Medicine* 28:108–15.

McMillen, M. M.
  1979   "Differential Mortality by Sex in Fetal and Neonatal Deaths." *Science* 204:89–91.

McPherson, B. D.
  1983   *Aging as a Social Process*. Toronto: Butterworths.
  1985   "The Meaning and Use of Time Across the Life-cycle: The Influence of Work, Family and Leisure." In E. M. Gee and G. M. Gutman (eds.), *Canadian Gerontological Collection V*. Winnipeg, Manitoba: The Canadian Association on Gerontology.

MacRae, H.
  1986   "Older Women and Identity Maintenance in Later Life." Paper presented at the annual meeting of the Canadian Association on Gerontology, Quebec City, November.

Madigan, F. C.
  1957   "Are Sex Mortality Differentials Biologically Caused?" *Milbank Memorial Fund Quarterly* 35:202–23.

Marcus, A. C., and T. E. Seeman
  1981a   "Sex Differences in Health Status: A Re-examination of the Nurturant Role Hypothesis." *American Sociological Review* 46:119–23.
  1981b   "Sex Differences in Reports of Illness and Disability: A Preliminary Test of the 'Fixed Role Obligations' Hypothesis." *Journal of Health and Social Behavior* 22:174–82.

Marcus, A. C., T. E. Seeman, and C. W. Telesk
  1982   "Sex Differences in Reports of Illness and Disability: A Further Test of the Fixed Role Hypothesis." *Social Science and Medicine* 17:993–1002.

Marcus, A. C., and J. M. Siegel
  1982   "Sex Differences in the Use of Physician Services: A Preliminary Test of the Fixed Role Hypothesis." *Journal of Health and Social Behavior* 23:186–97.

Marcus, L., and V. Jaeger
  1984   "The Elderly as Family Caregivers." *Canadian Journal on Aging* 3:33–43.

Marshall, J. R., D. I. Gregario, and D. Walsh
  1982   "Sex Differences in Illness Behavior: Care Seeking Among Cancer Patients." *Journal of Health and Social Behavior* 23:197–204.

Marshall, V. W.
  1980   "State of the Art Lecture: The Sociology of Aging." In J. Crawford (ed.), *Canadian Gerontological Collection III*. Winnipeg, Manitoba: The Canadian Association on Gerontology.

Mathiowetz, N. A., and R. M. Groves
  1985   "The Effects of Respondent Rules on Health Survey Reports." *American Journal of Public Health* 75:639–44.

Matthews, A. M.
  1986   "Widowhood as an Expectable Life Event." In V. W. Marshall (ed.), *Aging in Canada: Social Perspectives* (2nd. ed.). Don Mills, Ont.: Fitzhenry and Whiteside.

Matthews, A. M., and J. A. Tindale
  1987   "Retirement in Canada." In K. S. Markides and C. L. Cooper (eds.), *Retirement in Industralized Societies: Social, Psychological and Health Factors*. Sussex, England: Wiley.

Matthews, S. H., and J. Sprey
1984 "The Impact of Divorce on Grandparenthood: An Exploratory Study." *The Gerontologist* 24:41–47.

Mechanic, D.
1978 "Sex, Illness, Illness Behavior, and the Use of Health Services." *Social Science and Medicine* 12B:207–14.
1980 "Comment on Gove and Hughes." *American Sociological Review* 45:513–14.

Meissner, M., E. W. Humphreys, S. M. Meis, and W. J. Scheu
1975 "No Exit for Wives: Sexual Division of Labour and the Cumulation of Household Demands." *Canadian Review of Sociology and Anthropology* 12:424–39.

Miller, G. H., and D. R. Gerstein
1983 "The Life Expectancy of Nonsmoking Men and Women." *Public Health Reports* 98:343–49.

Moen, P.
1985 "Continuities and Discontinuities in Women's Labor Force Activities." In G.H. Elder, Jr. (ed.), *Life Course Dynamics: Trajectories and Transitions, 1968–1980*. Ithaca, N.Y.: Cornell University Press.

Morgan, L. A.
1984 "Continuity and Change in the Labour Force Activity of Recently Widowed Women." *The Gerontologist* 24:530–35.

Moss, M. S., S. Z. Moss, and E. L. Moles
1985 "The Quality of Relationships Between Elderly Parents and Their Out-of-town Children." *The Gerontologist* 25:134–40.

Mueller, C. B.
1985 "Surgery for Breast Cancer: Less May be as Good as More." *New England Journal of Medicine* 312:712–14.

Myles, J.
1982 "The Social Implications of Canada's Changing Age Structure." In G. M. Gutman (ed.), *Canada's Changing Age Structure: Implications for the Future*. Burnaby, B.C.: Simon Fraser University Publications.
1984 *Old Age in the Welfare State: The Political Economy of Public Pensions*. Boston, Mass.: Little, Brown.

Nadelson, C. C.
1984 "Geriatric Sex Problems: Discussion." *Journal of Geriatric Psychiatry* 17:139–48.

Nathanson, C. A.
1975 "Illness and the Feminine Role: A Theoretical Review." *Social Science and Medicine* 9:57–62.
1977 "Sex, Illness, and Medical Care: A Review of Data, Theory and Method." *Social Science and Medicine* 11:13–25.
1980 "Social Roles and Health Status among Women: The Significance of Employment." *Social Science and Medicine* 14A:463–71.

National Advisory Council on Aging
1986 "Community Support Services: Needs and Trends." *Expression* 3(2):2.

National Council of Welfare
1981 *Measuring Poverty: 1981 Poverty Lines*. Ottawa: National Council of Welfare.

1984a *1984 Poverty Lines*. Ottawa: National Council of Welfare.

1984b *Sixty-Five and Older: A Report by the National Council of Welfare on the Incomes of the Aged*. Ottawa: National Council of Welfare.

National Institutes of Health
1985 "Estrogen May Protect Against Lung Disorder." *Journal of the American Medical Association* 254(19):2721.

Nemschoff, H. L.
1981 "Women as Volunteers: Long History, New Roles." *Generations* 5:35, 48.

Nett, E.
1982 "A Call for Feminist Correctives to Research on Elders." *Resources for Feminist Research* 11:225–26.

Neugarten, B.L., V. Wood, R. J. Kraines, and B. Loomis
1963 "Women's Attitudes Towards the Menopause." *Vita Humana* 6:140–51.

Newman, E. S., S. R. Sherman, and C. E. Higgins
1982 "Retirement Expectations and Plans: A Comparison of Professional Men and Women." In M. Szinovacz (ed.), *Women's Retirement: Policy Implications of Recent Research*. Beverly Hills, Calif.: Sage.

Neysmith, S. M.
1984 "Poverty in Old Age: Can Pension Reform Meet the Needs of Women?" *Canadian Woman Studies* 5:17–21.

Northcott, H. C.
1984 "Widowhood and Remarriage Trends in Canada, 1956 to 1981." *Canadian Journal on Aging* 3:63–78.

Notelovitz, M., and M. Ware
1982 *Stand Tall: Every Woman's Guide to Preventing Osteoporosis*. New York: Bantam Books.

O'Rand, A. M., and J. C. Henretta
1982 "Delayed Career Entry, Industrial Pension Structure, and Early Retirement in a Cohort of Unmarried Women." *American Sociological Review* 47:365–73.

Palmore, E. B.
1965 "Differences in the Retirement Patterns of Men and Women." *The Gerontologist* 5:4–8.

Parsons, T.
1942 "Age and Sex in the Social Structure of the U.S." *American Sociological Review* 7:604–16.

Penfold, P. S.
1981 "Women and Depression." *Canadian Journal of Psychiatry* 26:24–31.

Penfold, P. S., and G. A. Walker
1983 *Women and the Psychiatric Paradox*. Montreal, Que.: Eden Press.

Perlmutter, M., and E. Hall
1985 *Adult Development and Aging*. New York: Wiley.

Perun, P. J., and D. D. V. Bielby
1981 "Towards a Model of Female Occupational Behavior: A Human Development Approach." *Psychology of Women Quarterly* 6:234–52.

Pfeiffer, E.
1974 "Sexuality and the Aging Individual." *Journal of the American Geriatric Society* 22:481–84.

Pfeiffer, E., and G. C. Davis
  1972 "Determinants of Sexual Behavior in Middle and Old Age." *Journal of the American Geriatrics Society* 20:151–58.

Pfeiffer, E., A. Verwoerdt, and H. S. Wang
  1968 "Sexual Behavior in Aged Men and Women: I. Observations on 254 Community Volunteers." *Archives of General Psychiatry* 19:753–58.

Phillips, D. L., and B. E. Segal
  1969 "Sexual Symptoms and Psychiatric Symptoms." *American Sociological Review* 34:58–72.

Piaget, J.
  1983 "Piaget's Theory." In W. Kessen (ed.), *History, Theory and Methods*. New York: Wiley.

Poggi, R. G., and D. I. Berland
  1985 "The Therapists' Reactions to the Elderly." *The Gerontologist* 25:508–13.

Porcino, J.
  1983 *Growing Older, Getting Better: A Handbook for Women in the Second Half of Life.* Reading, Mass.: Addison-Wesley.

Posner, J.
  1979 "It's All in Your Head: Feminist and Medical Models of Menopause (Strange Bedfellows)." *Sex Roles* 5:179–90.

Potts, D. M.
  1970 "Which is the Weaker Sex?" *Journal of Biosocial Science* (Supplement) 2:147–57.

Powell, L. S.
  1985 "Alzheimer's Disease: A Practical, Psychological Approach." In S. Golub and R. J. Freedman (eds.), *Health Needs of Women as They Age*. New York: Haworth Press.

Powers, E. A., and G. L. Bultena
  1976 "Sex Differences in Intimate Friendships in Old Age." *Journal of Marriage and the Family* 38:739–47.

Prentis, R. S.
  1980 "White Collar Working Women's Perceptions of Retirement." *The Gerontologist* 20:90–95.

Preston, S. H.
  1976 *Mortality Patterns in National Populations.* New York: Academic Press.
  1984 "Children and the Elderly: Divergent Paths for America's Dependents." *Demography* 21:435–56.

Price-Bonham, S., and C. K. Johnson
  1982 "Attitudes Toward Retirement: A Comparison of Professional and Nonprofessional Married Women." In M. Szinovacz (ed.), *Women's Retirement: Policy Implications of Recent Research*. Beverly Hills, Calif.: Sage.

Quinn, W. J.
  1983 "Personal and Family Adjustment in Later Life." *Journal of Marriage and the Family* 45:57–74.

Rasmuson, M.
  1971 "Men, the Weaker Sex?" *Impact of Science on Society* 21:43–54.

Recker, R. R., P. D. Saville, and R. R. Heaney
    1977   "Effect of Estrogens and Calcium on Bone Loss in Postmenopausal Women." *Annals of Internal Medicine* 87:649–55.

Renshaw, D. C.
    1984   "Geriatric Sex Problems." *Journal of Geriatric Psychiatry* 17:123–38.

Retherford, R. D.
    1975   *The Changing Sex Differential in Mortality.* Westport, Conn.: Greenwood.

Riegel, K.
    1975   "Toward a Dialectical Theory of Development." *Human Development* 18:50–64.

Riggs, B. L., E. Seeman, S. F. Hodgson, D. R. Taves, and W. M. O'Fallon
    1982   "Effect of the Fluoride/Calcium Regimen on Vertebral Fracture Occurrence in Postmenopausal Osteoporosis." *New England Journal of Medicine* 306:446–50.

Riley, M. W., M. Johnson, and A. Foner
    1972   *Aging and Society: Volume 3. A Sociology of Age Stratificiation.* New York: Russel Sage Foundation.

Roberto, K. A., and J. P. Scott
    1984–85 "Friendship Patterns Among Older Women." *International Journal of Aging and Human Development* 19:1–10.
    1986   "Equity Considerations in the Friendships of Older Adults." *Journal of Gerontology* 41:241–47.

Roberts, W. L.
    1980   "Significant Elements in the Relationship of Long-married Couples." *International Journal of Aging and Human Development* 10:265–72.

Robertson, J. F.
    1977   "Grandmotherhood: A Study of Role Conception." *Journal of Marriage and the Family* 39:165–74.

Rodin, J.
    1983   "Behavioral Medicine: Beneficial Effects of Self-control Training in the Aged." *International Review of Applied Psychology* 32:153–81.

Roebuck, J.
    1983   "Grandma as Revolutionary: Elderly Women and Some Modern Patterns of Social Change." *International Journal of Aging and Human Development* 17:249–66.

Root, N., and J. R. Daley
    1980   "Are Women Safer Workers? A New Look at the Data." *Monthly Labor Review* 103:3–10.

Rosenthal, C. J.
    1985   "Kinkeeping in the Familial Division of Labor." *Journal of Marriage and the Family* 47:965–74.
    1986a "Family Supports in Later Life: Does Ethnicity Make a Difference?" *The Gerontologist* 26:19–24.
    1986b "The Differentiation of Multigenerational Households." *Canadian Journal on Aging* 5:27–42.

Rosenthal, S. H.
    1968   "The Involutional Depressive Syndrome." *American Journal of Psychiatry* (Supplement) 124:21–25.

Rossi, A.
  1980   "Life-span Theories and Women's Lives." *Signs* 6:4–32.
Rubin, L.
  1979   *Women of a Certain Age: The Mid-life Search for Self.* New York: Harper and Row.
Ruzicka, L. T., and A. D. Lado
  1983   "Sex Differentials in Mortality: Conclusions and Prospects." In A. D. Lado and L. T. Ruzicka (eds.), *Sex Differentials in Mortality: Trends, Determinants and Consequences.* Canberra: Australian National University Press.
Schaie, K. W.
  1973   "Methodological Problems in Descriptive Developmental Research on Adulthood and Aging." In J. R. Nesselroade and H. W. Reese (eds.), *Life-Span Development Psychology: Methodological Issues.* New York: Academic Press.
  1977   "Quasi-experimental Research Designs in the Psychology of Aging." In J. E. Birren and K. W. Schaie (eds.), *Handbook of the Psychology of Aging.* New York: Van Nostrand Reinhold.
Schulz, R.
  1980   "Aging and Control." In J. Gardner and M. E. P. Seligman (eds.), *Human Helplessness: Theory and Applications.* New York: Academic Press.
Schulz, R., and G. Brenner
  1977   "Relocation of the Aged: A Review and Theoretical Analysis." *Journal of Gerontology* 32:323–33.
Sekaran, U.
  1986   "Significant Differences in Quality-of-life Factors and Their Correlates: Differences in Career Orientation or Gender?" *Sex Roles* 14:261–79.
Shanas, E.
  1979   "Social Myth as Hypothesis: The Case of the Family Relations of Older People." *The Gerontologist* 19:3–9.
Shapiro, S., J. P. Kelly, L. Rosenberg, D. W. Kaufman, S. P. Helmrich, N. B. Rosenshein, *et al.*
  1985   "Risk of Localized and Widespread Endometrial Cancer in Relation to Recent and Discontinued Use of Conjugated Estrogens." *New England Journal of Medicine* 313:969–72.
Shaw, L. B.
  1984   "Retirement Plans of Middle-aged Married Women." *The Gerontologist* 24:154–59.
Siegel, J. S.
  1980   "Balancing the Sexes." *American Demographics* 2:4, 50.
Silverman, P. R., and A. Cooperband
  1975   "On Widowhood: Mutual Help and the Elderly Widow." *Journal of Geriatric Psychiatry* 8:9–27.
Singh, B. K., and J. S. Williams
  1981   "Childlessness and Family Satisfaction." *Research on Aging* 3:218–27.
Slovic, P.
  1966   "Risk-taking in Children: Age and Sex Differences." *Child Development* 37:169–76.

Smith, D. C., R. Prentice, D. J. Thompson, and W. L. Herrmann
  1975   "Association of Exogenous Estrogen and Endometrial Carcinoma." *New England Journal of Medicine* 293:1164–67.

Snyder, E., and E. Spreitzer
  1976   "Attitudes of the aged Toward Non-traditional Sexual Behavior." *Archives of Sexual Behavior* 5:249–54.

Sontag, S.
  1972   "The Double Standard of Aging." *Saturday Review* September 23:29–38.

Spanier, G. B., and R. A. Lewis
  1980   "Marital Quality: A Review of the Seventies." *Journal of Marriage and the Family* 42:825–39.

Spar, J. E.
  1982   "Dementia in the Aged." *Psychiatric Clinics of North America* 5:67–86.

Spletter, M.
  1982   *A Woman's Choice: New Options in the Treatment of Breast Cancer.* Boston: Beacon Press.

Stadel, B. V., and N. Weiss
  1975   "Characteristics of Menopausal Women: A Survey of King and Pierce Counties in Washington, 1973–1974." *American Journal of Epidemiology* 102:209–16.

Statistics Canada
  1981   *The Health of Canadians: Report of the Canada Health Survey.* Ottawa: Statistics Canada Catalogue No. 82-538E.
  1982   *Pension Plans in Canada, 1980.* Ottawa: Statistics Canada Catalogue No. 74-401.
  1984a   *Mental Health Statistics: Mental and Psychiatric Hospitals, 1980–81 and 1981–82.* Ottawa: Statistics Canada Catalogue No. 83-204.
  1984b   *The Elderly in Canada.* Ottawa: Statistics Canada Catalogue No. 99-932.
  1985   *Income Distributions by Size in Canada, 1983.* Ottawa: Statistics Canada Catalogue No. 13-207.

Stenback, A.
  1980   "Depression and Suicidal Behavior in Old Age." In J. E. Birren and R. B. Sloane (eds.), *Handbook of Mental Health and Aging.* Englewood Cliffs, N.J.: Prentice-Hall.

Stinnett, N., L. M. Carter, and J. E. Montgomery
  1972   "Older Persons' Perceptions of Their Marriages." *Journal of Marriage and the Family* 34:665–70.

Stone, L. O., and S. Fletcher
  1980   *A Profile of Canada's Older Population.* Montreal: Institute for Research on Public Policy.

Stoppard, J. M., S. E. Ulch, and A. Oakley
  1986   "Sex Differences in Depression: An Evaluation of Current Perspectives." Paper presented at the annual meeting of the Canadian Psychological Association, Toronto, June.

Storm, C., T. Storm, and J. Strike-Schurman
  1985   "Obligations for Care: Beliefs in a Small Canadian Town." *Canadian Journal on Aging* 4:75–85.

Storrie, V. J.
  1977   *Male and Female Car Drivers: Differences Observed in Accidents.* Berkshire, England: Accident Investigation Division, Safety Department, Crowthorne Transport and Road Research Laboratory.
Streib, G. F., and R. W. Beck
  1980   "Older Families: A Decade Review." *Journal of Marriage and the Family* 42:937–56.
Szalai, A.
  1975   "Women's Time: Women in Light of Contemporary Time-budget Research." *Future*: 385–99.
Szinovacz, M.
  1982a "Personal Problems and Adjustment to Retirement." In M. Szinovacz (ed.), *Women's Retirement: Policy Implications of Recent Research.* Beverly Hills, Calif.: Sage.
  1982b "Retirement Plans and Retirement Adjustment." In M. Szinovacz (ed.), *Women's Retirement: Policy Implications of Recent Research.* Beverly Hills, Calif.: Sage.
  1983   "Beyond the Hearth: Older Women and Retirement." In E. W. Markson (ed.), *Older Women: Issues and Prospects.* Lexington, Mass.: Lexington Books.
Thomas, K., and A. Wister
  1984   "Living Arrangements of Older Women: The Ethnic Dimension." *Journal of Marriage and the Family* 46:301–11.
Thomas, L.
  1982   "Sexuality and Aging: Essential Vitamin or Popcorn?" *The Gerontologist* 22:240–43.
Thompson, M. K., and J. S. Brown
  1980   "Feminine Roles and Variations in Women's Illness Behaviors." *Pacific Sociological Review* 23:405–22.
Tindale, J. A., J. Edwardh, and S. Neysmith
  1983   "Distributional Justice and Income Security for the Canadian Aged: Background Paper." Paper presented at the annual meeting of the Canadian Association on Gerontology, Winnipeg.
Traupmann, J.
  1982   "Intimacy in Older Women's Lives." *The Gerontologist* 22:493–98.
  1984   "Does Sexuality Fade Over Time? A Look at the Question and the Answer." *Journal of Geriatric Psychiatry* 17:149–59.
Trela, J. E., and D. J. Jackson
  1979   "Family Life and Community Participation in Old Age." *Research on Aging* 1:233–52.
Uhlenberg, P., and M. A. D. Myers
  1981   "Divorce and the Elderly." *The Gerontologist* 21:276–82.
Vance, B. K., and V. Green
  1984   "Lesbian Identities: An Examination of Sexual Behavior and Sex Role Attribution as Related to Age of Initial Same-Sex Sexual Encounter." *Psychology of Women Quarterly* 8:293–307.
van de Walle, E.
  1976   "Household Dynamics in a Belgian Village, 1874–1886." *Family History* 1:80–94.

Veevers, J. E.
    1985   Personal communication.
    1986   "The Lion's Share: Relative Contributions of Husbands and Wives in Two-income Families." Paper presented at the annual meeting of the Canadian Sociology and Anthropology Association, Winnipeg, June.

Veevers, J. E., and E. M. Gee
    1986   "Playing It Safe: Accident Mortality and Gender Roles." *Sociological Focus* 19:349–60.

Verbrugge, L. M.
    1976   "Sex Differentials in Morbidity and Mortality in the United States." *Social Biology* 23:276–96.
    1979a   "Female Illness Rates and Illness Behavior: Testing Hypotheses about Sex Differences in Health." *Women and Health* 4:61–79.
    1979b   "Marital Status and Health." *Journal of Marriage and the Family* 41:267–85.
    1980   "Comment on Walter R. Gove and Michael Hughes, 'Possible Causes of the Apparent Sex Differences in Physical Health.' " *American Sociological Review* 45:507–12.
    1982   "Women's Social Roles and Health." In P. W. Berman and E. R. Ramey (eds.), *Women: A Developmental Perspective*. Washington, D.C.: U.S. Department of Health and Human Services, NIH Publication No. 82-2298.
    1983   "Women and Men: Mortality and Health of Older People." In M. W. Riley, B. B. Hess, and K. Bond (eds.), *Aging in Society: Selected Reviews of Recent Research*. Hillsdale, N.J.: Laurence Erlbaum.
    1985   "Gender and Health: An Update of Hypotheses and Evidence." *Journal of Health and Social Behavior* 26:156–82.

Verbrugge, L. M., and R. P. Steiner
    1981   "Physician Treatment of Men and Women Patients: Sex Bias or Appropriate Care?" *Medical Care* 19:609–32.

Verwoerdt, A., E. Pfeiffer, and H. S. Wang
    1969   "Sexual Behavior in Senescence: II. Patterns of Sexual Activity and Interest." *Geriatrics* 24:137–54.

Waldron, I.
    1976   "Why do Women Live Longer than Men?" *Journal of Human Stress* 2:2–13.
    1980   "Employment and Women's Health: An Analysis of Causal Relationships." *International Journal of Health Services* 10:435–54.
    1982   "An Analysis of Causes of Sex Differences in Mortality and Morbidity." In W. R. Gove and G. R. Carpenter (eds.), *The Fundamental Connection between Nature and Nurture*. Lexington, Mass.: Lexington Books.
    1983   "The Role of Genetic and Biological Factors in Sex Differences in Mortality." In A. D. Lopez and L. T. Ruzicka (eds.), *Sex Differentials in Mortality: Trends, Determinants and Consequences*. Canberra: Australian National University Press.

Waldron, I., H. Herold, D. Dunn, and R. Staum
    1982   "Reciprocal Effects of Health and Labor Force Participation among Women: Evidence from Two Longitudinal Studies." *Journal of Occupational Medicine* 24:127–32.

Walker, A. J., and L. Thompson
  1983   "Intimacy and Intergenerational Aid and Contact Among Mothers and Daughters." *Journal of Marriage and the Family* 45:841–49.
Wallen, J., H. Waitzkin, and J. D. Stoeckle
  1979   "Physician Stereotypes about Female Health and Illness: A Study of Patient's Sex and the Information Process during Medical Interviews." *Women and Health* 4:135–46.
Ward, R., S. Sherman, and M. LaGory
  1984   "Subjective Network Assessments and Subjective Well-being." *Journal of Gerontology* 39:93–101.
Wasow, M., and M. B. Loeb
  1978   "Sexuality in Nursing Homes." In R. Solnick (ed.), *Sexuality and Aging*. Los Angeles: University of Southern California Press.
Weber, F., R. J. Burnard, and D. Roy
  1983   "Effects of a High-Complex-Carbohydrate, Low-Fat Diet and Daily Exercise in Individuals 70 Years of Age and Older." *Journal of Gerontology*, 38:155–61.
Weg, R.
  1983   "The Physiological Perspective." In R. Weg (ed.), *Sexuality in Later Years: Roles and Behaviors*. New York: Academic Press.
Weiss, N. S., C. L. Ure, J. H. Ballard, A. R. Williams, and J. R. Daling
  1980   "Decreased Risk of Fractures of the Hip and Lower Forearm with Post-menopausal Use of Estrogen." *New England Journal of Medicine* 303:1195–98.
Whedon, G. D.
  1981   "Osteoporosis." *New England Journal of Medicine* 305:397–99.
White, C. B.
  1982   "Sexual Interest, Attitudes, Knowledge, and Sexual History in Relation to Sexual Behavior in the Institutionalized Aged." *Archives of Sexual Behavior* 11:11–21.
Wilson, J., W. J. Weikel, and H. Rose
  1982   "A Comparison of Nontraditional and Traditional Career Women." *Vocational Guidance Quarterly* 31:109–17.
Wilson, R. A.
  1966   *Forever Feminine*. New York: M. Evans.
Wilson, R., and I. Wilson
  1963   "The Fate of the Nontreated Postmenopausal Woman: A Plea for the Maintenance of Adequate Estrogen from Puberty to Grave." *Journal of the American Geriatrics Society* 11:347–62.
Winokur, G.
  1973   "Depression in the Menopause." *American Journal of Psychiatry* 130:92–93.
Wister, A. V.
  1985   "Living Arrangement Choices Among the Elderly." *Canadian Journal on Aging* 4:127–44.
Wister, A. V., and L. Strain
  1986   "Social Support and Well-being: A Comparison of Older Widows and Widowers." Paper presented at the annual meeting of the Canadian Sociology and Anthropology Association, Winnipeg, June.

Wiswell, R. A.
   1980   "Relaxation, Exercise, and Aging." In J. E. Birren and R. B. Sloane (eds.), *Handbook of Mental Health and Aging*. Englewood Cliffs, N.J.: Prentice-Hall.
Wolinsky, F. D., and M. E. Zusman
   1981   "Sex and Health: A New Look at an Old Relationship." Paper presented at the annual meeting of the American Sociological Association, Toronto, August.
Wood, V., and J. F. Robertson
   1978   "Friendship and Kinship Interaction: Differential Effect on the Morale of the Elderly." *Journal of Marriage and the Family* 40:367–75.
Wyshak, G.
   1981   "Hip Fracture in Elderly Women and Reproductive History." *Journal of Gerontology* 36:424–27.
Yalom, M., S. Estler, and W. Brewster
   1982   "Changes in Female Sexuality: A Study in Mother/Daughter Communication and Generational Differences." *Psychology of Women Quarterly* 7:141–54.
Ziel, H. K., and W. D. Finkle
   1975   "Increased Risk of Endometrial Carcinoma among Users of Conjugated Estrogens." *New England Journal of Medicine* 293:1167–70.

INDEX